CISNEROS

CISNEROS

Portrait of a
New American

by

KEMPER DIEHL

and

JAN JARBOE

With 56 pages of photographs

CORONA
PUBLISHING
COMPANY
San Antonio, Texas
1985

Library of Congress Cataloging in Publication Data

Diehl, Kemper.
    Cisneros : portrait of a new American.

    Includes index.
    1. Cisneros, Henry. 2. San Antonio (Tex.)--Mayors--
Biography. 3. San Antonio (Tex.)--Politics and
government. I. Jarboe, Jan, 1951-   . II. Title.
F394.S2C563 1985   976.4'351063'0924 [B] 84-72834
ISBN 0-931722-35-7
ISBN 0-931722-37-3 (pbk.)

Printed and bound in the United States of America

Title page photo by Scott Sines
Book design by James J. Fox

Foreword

The first time I saw Henry Cisneros' name it appeared on my appointment calendar on a day early in the fall of 1971. I was then Secretary of Health, Education, and Welfare. He was a new White House Fellow. The appointment had been scheduled so that we could look each other over in anticipation of his assignment to my department.

I knew in advance that Henry Cisneros would prove to be an impressive young man. He was, after all, one of about twenty White House Fellows selected from a field of more than 2,500 applicants. I had worked with other White House Fellows in previous years; they were all impressive. Nothing I yet knew, however, prepared me for just how impressive Henry Cisneros would turn out to be.

I liked him from the first moment we met. Although only twenty-four years old, he had the maturity that could only have come from considerable experience. He also had warmth, charm, and humor. His intelligence was as self-evident as his good looks. But what most impressed me was his air of quiet confidence—the outward reflection, I was sure, of an inner sense of balance.

I came to know Henry well during the course of the ensuing year. I saw how he handled himself in a variety of situations. He was cool under pressure. He kept a clear and steady eye on the merits of the issues he was dealing with. His inner balance wheel—gyroscope might be a better word—made him remarkably surefooted. He didn't make mistakes.

Because White House Fellows have very full schedules, including long trips (Henry's group went to Africa and Asia) and briefings with such bigwigs as Congressional leaders and Cabinet members, the official to whom a Fellow is assigned normally gives her or him staff functions not subject to rigorous deadlines. Until Henry came along, that was my own practice also. He quickly showed me, however, that he could follow through quickly and efficiently with such demanding projects as the development of a strategy for the delivery of HEW services in cities, or the preparation of an important speech. Everything I got from him was well thought through, well researched, and well written.

All of this is part of the reason why, one day near the close of his tour of duty at HEW when he and I were talking about his future plans, I told him that I saw him as a "national resource." I was also alluding, of course, to his Spanish-speaking background. Hispanic-Americans had not then—and have not yet—achieved representation in the nation's leadership in a proportion anywhere near commensurate with their importance to our society. It took no special discernment on my part to see that Henry Cisneros had the potential to play a major role in helping to fill this void. His personal assets and his ethnic background constituted a God-given combination. With hard work, discipline, and a fair share of luck, the sky would be the limit for his political future. To fulfill it he would need above all the surefootedness that had already served him so well.

In his steady progress from the San Antonio City Council to the Mayoralty and from City Hall to the national stage, this attribute has in fact been indispensable. Many examples might serve, but the most conspicuous surely is the manner in which he has walked the line between the requirement of responding to and speaking for the Hispanic community of San Antonio and the need to enlist and retain the support of the city's business leaders. Too little zeal on behalf of the former would damn him as the Chicano version of an "Uncle Tom;" too much militancy would lead the latter to question his "soundness." This book unfolds in fascinating detail the story of his success in expanding and consolidating his support among both groups.

To the casual observer, such an achievement may seem easy. It is in fact easy only in the sense that any disciplined performance—a well-played piano sonata, for example, or a smoothly executed double-play—is easy. Henry's performance has given new life to one of my favorite observations: that politics is the most difficult of the arts and the noblest of the professions.

If in 1972 Henry Cisneros was already a national resource, the intervening years have made him even more so. No politician could ask for a more demanding challenge, and yet to manage such a challenge without letting it become more of a burden than a satisfaction demands a well-developed sense either of humor or of perspective. (Is there a difference?) Henry, fortunately, is well endowed with both. I have no doubt, moreover, that the same qualities that have brought him his present success will, with a little continued luck, carry him farther—perhaps much farther.

In whatever he does, Henry Cisneros will have to live with the awareness that he is a champion and a role model for a minority that has suffered deprivation as well as discrimination. What attributes are thereby required of him? Understanding, first of all, of the minority's needs and aspirations and the ability to articulate them. What else? Courage, surely, and tenacity coupled with the capacity to generate trust. And leadership—leadership linked to sensitivity toward the larger community. Indeed, the ultimate contribution of such leadership is to enable the group to feel less like a minority and more like a part of that larger community. This may yet be Henry Cisneros' most important contribution to the nation's Latin-Americans.

Time and circumstance will, of course, have much to say about how far Henry Cisneros succeeds in realizing his potential. As to this I cannot offer a confident prediction. But of one thing I am certain: that whatever time and circumstance allow Henry Cisneros to do will be accomplished with dignity and grace. And one thing more—that any reader of this book will come away from the experience with a share of this same certainty.

December 10, 1984   Elliot L. Richardson
Boston, Massachusetts

Contents

Acknowledgments

In writing this book we have been fortunate to have help from many people who gave generously of time and information. In particular we are grateful for the encouragement and assistance of our colleagues at the San Antonio *Express-News*. Charles O. Kilpatrick, editor and publisher, demonstrated his interest and friendship in many ways and his help was essential to what success we have achieved. We also want to thank Bert Wise, executive editor, and Sterlin Holmsley, editorial director. Others at the newspapers who were helpful include Librarian Judy Zipp, Cartoonist John Branch, and all the photographers whose work appears in this book. We especially thank J. B. Hazlett, whose photograph of Henry Cisneros on election night in 1981 appears on the cover.

We would never have completed the project at all, of course, without the support of our spouses, Suzanne Diehl and Clinton Rabb. They encouraged us to begin the project, were patient with the inevitable disruptions it created, and cheered us on during the final deadline pressures.

The effort could not have succeeded without the cooperation of Henry G. Cisneros and his wife, Mary Alice. The mayor somehow made time in his crowded schedule for extensive interviews. His father and mother, Colonel and Mrs. George Cisneros, were especially helpful, as was his brother, George, Jr., and his wife, Catherine.

Ruben and Romulo Munguia, the mayor's uncles, helped with their recollections of family and political history, and B. K. Munguia, the mayor's cousin, freely granted us access to her Yale University thesis on their grandfather, Romulo Munguia, Sr. (The reader will notice that we elected not to use accent marks on Spanish surnames, since neither the Munguia family nor the Cisneros family uses written accents as a matter of course.)

Special thanks go to Robert D. Sohn, who generously provided Jan a nurturing place to write, and to his assistant, Hope Wilson Brans, who answered telephones and transcribed taped interviews.

We have drawn extensively on the work of many reporters who have written about Cisneros over the years. We would particularly like to thank freelance writer Rick Casey, formerly of the *Express-News* and *SA* magazine, and James McCrory, veteran political reporter for the *Express-News*.

Dr. George Shipley, a pollster and political consultant with deep understanding of Texas and U.S. politics, was among the first to urge us to undertake this assignment, and he shared information and insights throughout the process. Jim Dublin, a public relations executive, was also most helpful.

Former Mayor Lila Cockrell gave us the benefit of her wisdom concerning the development of the mayor's office. U.S. Representative Albert Bustamante, as always, was helpful in providing information about politics in South Texas.

We would also like to thank Richard G. Santos for providing background of the period of San Antonio history when thousands of refugees from political turmoil came to San Antonio from Mexico. Clarence LaRoche helped with recollections of the elder Munguia. Others who were helpful were Lane Stephenson and Wayne Stark of Texas A&M University, Trinity University President Ronald Calgaard, Dr. Tucker Gibson, political science professor at Trinity, and Jess Poston, assistant general manager of City Public Service.

Shirl Thomas, Barbie Hernandez, Delzie Madkins, and Francis Rios in the mayor's office went out of their way to help us with information and assistance. We thank the mayor's overworked staff. White House Photo Editor Barry Fernald generously provided photographs. Alice Evett, Corona's tireless editor, caught small and not-so-small errors that evaded all the rest of us.

Finally, we are indebted to publisher David Bowen who had the idea for this book and who has worked cheerfully and patiently at the tasks of editing and prodding us to completion.

CISNEROS

Portrait of a
New American

I

Who Is Henry?
What Is He?

Grinning like a big-leaguer, Henry Cisneros strolled down Walter Mondale's driveway on July 4, 1984, and steeled himself to face the national press.

At 37, this two-term mayor of San Antonio was about to be interviewed for the Democratic nomination for the vice presidency of the United States. Even his mother thought he was too young for the job.

Partly due to his familiarity with Mondale, whom he had endorsed eighteen months before, but more because of his own innate self-confidence, Cisneros was not nervous prior to his vice presidential interview. In fact, the inner-city boy from Texas, son of an Army colonel, looked forward to the time alone with the minister's son and farm boy from Minnesota.

"It will be politician-to-politician with Mondale and me," Cisneros said during the flight up from San Antonio. "The stressful part of this trip will be facing the national press."

There was not a trace of stress or strain on Cisneros' face as he walked down Mondale's shady, wooded driveway with his wife, Mary Alice, and their two young daughters. Tall, lanky, and lean, Cisneros ambled towards the waiting microphones and prepared to be nationalized.

To the members of the press who had staked out in Mondale's mosquito-infested subdivision for three weeks, Cisneros was just another pretty face on parade. The seventh pretty face to be exact. One by one, three women, two black mayors, and one white male had filed into Mondale's cabin-like home to be interviewed for the vice presidency.

By July 4, the press had the veepstakes routine down pat. Day after day, the drill went like this:

Reporters loaded into vans at McGuire's Inn, a comfortable but not extravagant hotel in nearby St. Paul. They cracked jokes during the 20-minute ride to Mondale's house in North Oaks. Once there, they piled out of the vans under the disapproving gaze of the neighbors who despised the daily invasion into their rural seclusion. Then they rushed to set up equipment near a Secret Service trailer parked outside Mondale's house. While waiting for the latest vice presidential hopeful to arrive, they cooled their heels impatiently. There was always a brief photo opportunity before Mondale and the prospective veep wandered behind closed doors to talk shop. Then the reporters went back to McGuire's to continue their stakeout in style—usually over breakfast or a swim. When the time was right, Mondale's campaign staff loaded the reporters on the van and took them back to the house for a 20-minute press conference.

It had been Cisneros' idea to bring his two young daughters along. Mary Alice had argued against it on grounds it would be too much pressure on Theresa, 13, and Mercedes, 8. But Cisneros said it would be a Fourth of July the girls would always remember.

Mary Alice carried a basket filled with bluebonnet suckers, jalapeno candy, and a sugar model of the Alamo. The girls, wearing new dresses and white ankle socks

2

trimmed with lace, managed to smile naturally while mosquitoes munched on their legs. During the photo opportunity, Cisneros tried unsuccessfully to describe the taste of jalapeno candy to the national press corps.

Mondale interrupted to tell reporters he would personally present a piece of the candy to the winners of a July 4th softball game between the Secret Service and the press.

"The loser gets two pieces," cracked one network cameraman.

The Cisneros family, vivid and dark-haired, struck an unfamiliar, arresting note to most of the journalists on holiday duty in Mondale's driveway. Sure, the reporters realized an estimated 14 million Hispanics are citizens of the United States. They knew Hispanics are the hottest ethnic group to watch in the 1980's. However, since Hispanics are concentrated in Sunbelt cities and the national press hugs the East Coast, Mexican-Americans like Cisneros are still a mysterious sight at political center stage.

So it happened that the first words spoken to Cisneros during the brief photo session came from a network cameraman who called out cheerfully: "Buenos dias, Mayor Cisneros."

The greeting surprised San Antonio reporters who had long ago stopped dwelling on Cisneros' ethnicity. For a split second, it seemed to throw Cisneros off center but he soon regained his political balance.

"Buenos dias," Cisneros replied, quickly adding with an infectious smile, "and Happy Fourth of July."

If there were ever any doubt that American politics is no longer the purview of Anglo-Saxon males, the fact that Mondale interviewed only one—Senator Lloyd Bentsen of Texas—for the vice presidency is proof that the drive for power by women, blacks, and Hispanics has permanently altered the voting balance in this country.

Cisneros did not leap ahead of his political peers only

3

because he is a bright, articulate, exciting young politician. He is the right Hispanic at the right time, and he's riding the same wave that Ferraro and the Reverend Jackson rode in 1984.

In 1974, there were only 2,991 black elected officials at all levels of government in this country. Ten years later, the number of blacks holding elective office had almost doubled to 5,700.

In 1973, 16 of 535 members of Congress were women. In 1983, the number of females in Congress had increased to 23. The number of women in state legislatures in 1973 was 425 out of 7,563, or 5.6 percent. Ten years later, 992 out of 7,438 or 13.3 percent of all state legislators were women.

In Texas, the number of Mexican-American elected officials increased from 862 in 1974 to 1,371 in 1984.

The point of the numbers is that Ferraro, Jackson, and Cisneros did not arrive at center stage in the Democratic Party in 1984 on the strength of their own persuasion. They were pushed by a bottom-up movement of women and minorities.

Ethnically, Cisneros is Mexican-American. He lives in the tension between two cultures, just as his parents did as they balanced the demands of military life with their day-to-day domestic life in a middle-class Mexican-American neighborhood in San Antonio.

"Thanks to my parents, who never moved out of the West Side, I never lost respect for the community or understanding of basic problems," Cisneros said during one of the interviews for this book. "When you live on Monterey Street, which is only three streets north of really poor areas, you know just how close the line is; how shallow the ice is. We may be living on a veneer of prosperity, but the West Side still looks like a forever-extending barrio."

Intellectually, he is a philosopher-pragmatist. With a master's degree from Harvard and a Ph.D. from George Washington University, Cisneros has combined the roles of scholar and politician. He has a Platonic view of government—he believes certain people of good will and extraordinary intelligence have a duty or mission to lead. On the other hand, his own leadership style is to paint a concrete image—such as a vision of San Antonio as a high-technology production and employment center— and then sit down and write a step-by-step manual filled with technical jargon and a specific timetable.

Politically, he is a middle-of-the-road Democrat. In the 1984 Democratic primary, he supported former U.S. Representative Bob Krueger against Lloyd Doggett, the liberal in the race, and Kent Hance, the conservative. He supports U.S. Senator Lloyd Bentsen. He mistrusts extremists.

Emotionally, he is high-strung: energetic, driving, persistent, impatient, sometimes even petulant. Fourteen-hour workdays are the rule with Cisneros, not the exception. He is mystified by people who do not thrive on meritocracy, as he does, and the idea of losing infuriates and terrifies him. In a fit of anger, he once submitted— then later withdrew—a letter of resignation from the San Antonio City Council after losing a bid to be mayor pro tem.

Most of his displays of righteous indignation only boost his popularity. One of the fondest memories many San Antonians have of Cisneros was when he angrily refused to ride in an important parade during Fiesta week because parade officials informed him at the last minute that his wife and two daughters could not ride with him. On another occasion, Cisneros went wild with anger over the senseless death of a blind man, beaten to death by young punks who stole the man's three-dollar radio. Cisneros led media tours through the old man's rat-infested, dilapidated neighborhood shouting as he paced up and down the streets, "I want this block! I want this block cleaned up!"

How did it happen that Cisneros, a virtually untested   5

political commodity with only one contested race under his belt, jumped ahead of all his Democratic peers in Texas and the Southwest? How did someone with limited traditional political experience come in second behind Congresswoman Geraldine Ferraro as Mondale's choice for a running mate? Why were buttons that said "Cisneros: The Future" selling faster than they could be printed at the 1984 Democratic National Convention?

——— Despite his age and lack of positioning within the national Democratic Party, Cisneros was a serious candidate for the vice presidency in 1984 because he was the physical embodiment of two powerful modern political impulses—the immigrant story and the New America.

To date, these two impulses have weakened each other in the competition for dominance. In 1984, the tug-of-war played itself out in the Democratic presidential battle between Walter Mondale, heir to the New Deal coalition which brought immigrants into the mainstream, and Gary Hart, the neoliberal whose campaign theme of "new ideas" made heroes out of risk-taking entrepreneurs, not the hopeful masses of America's new arrivals.*

If the so-called immigrant storytellers and the neoliberals ever get together it will be someone like Cisneros who bridges the wide gap between these two political movements. By accident of timing and birth, Cisneros has one foot in either camp. He's a New Dealer born during the baby boom. Try as he may, Cisneros has not escaped the conclusion of his generation: The old solutions don't work anymore; America needs new ideas.

Cisneros is a future-oriented, heavy-thinker from the heart of New America's Sunbelt whose Mexican revolutionary grandfather crossed the border into Texas with 18 cents in his pocket in 1924. On the day he was interviewed

---

*Richard Reeves, a syndicated columnist, described this philosophical split in the Democratic Party in an August 1984 story in the *New York Times Magazine*.

for the vice presidency, Cisneros told his own immigrant story.

"When my grandfather crossed into Texas from Mexico, he could never have imagined that someday one of his own would be interviewed for the vice presidency of the United States," Cisneros said. "The fact that this is happening is a testimony to the openness of American society and is proof that if we have faith in people and give them the tools to work with, they will achieve."

This immigrant's grandson is a graduate of Harvard's John F. Kennedy School of Government, one of the new generation of urbanologists who are professionally trained for politics. By day, he runs San Antonio as though he were the chief executive officer of a futuristic company, but every night he touches base with his past. He and his family live in a five-room, gray frame house once owned by his grandfather that is located in the heart of a middle-class Mexican-American neighborhood on San Antonio's West Side.

Cisneros identifies strongly with the image of the Democratic Party as the home of immigrants. When he hears New York Governor Mario Cuomo describe his father's arrival at Ellis Island, his mental compass is fixed on the Rio Grande and the vivid image of thousands of Mexican-Americans crossing into Texas each year in search of work and a new life.

Cisneros realized that as the first Mexican-American ever to be interviewed for the vice presidency it was important for him to acknowledge other ethnic groups. When the national press asked him if black voters would be slighted if he were selected as Mondale's running mate, Cisneros was ready for the question.

"My presence here today," Cisneros said, "is a testimony to the changing-work the black civil rights leaders did in the 1960's. The successes that Americans who are categorized—women, the aged, the handicapped, and Hispanics—are enjoying today are in large measure due

7

to the sacrifices and breakthroughs of the black community."

With those words, Cisneros hoped to make it clear that when push came to shove the national leader of Hispanics would stand with the New Dealers and the immigrants, not the yuppies.

"If you ever want to know what I'm likely to do on an issue, just remember that I'm never going to stray too far from my Mexican-American base," Cisneros told us during an interview.

Push doesn't come to shove very often with Cisneros. He prides himself on being a bridge-builder, which is how he's gotten so far so fast without the wear and tear Jackson endured to gain a national voice.

"Everybody ought to make the strongest case they can—blacks, Hispanics, women, conservatives, liberals. Everybody must demand their say, but not their way," Cisneros said in conversation about his own vice presidential chances. "It will kill the Democratic Party if everybody insists on having it their own way."

Besides, there is a twist to his own philosophy about minority politics that makes him an ally of the neoliberals, as well as of conservative businessmen. Cisneros wants to change the agenda so that minority politicians are not dealing exclusively with social programs, voting rights, and police brutality but instead are concentrating their energies on economic development in the private sector. His "double-fisted" approach of government and the private sector working together to create jobs for the unemployed sometimes gets him crosswise with both conservatives and liberals. Conservatives sometimes criticize him for supporting government programs. Liberals sometimes mistrust him for being a cheerleader for the free enterprise system.

Economic development is almost a religion with Cisneros. All over the country, he has preached that government's job is to work with private industry to create

8

jobs for people who've been trapped in the cycle of poverty.

His ideas about economic development appeal to Republicans as well as Democrats. Cisneros does not believe all of supply side economics is evil. He is a Democrat who prefers tax incentives to bailouts and loans as a vehicle for revitalizing the decaying industries of the "rustbelt."

Until he was appointed to serve on President Reagan's Bipartisan Commission on Central America, many national political players were unaware of his strong identification with the Democratic Party. City Council candidates run as non-partisans in San Antonio and Cisneros had kept a low profile as a Democrat.

One who was surprised was former Secretary of the Department of Health, Education, and Welfare Elliot Richardson, for whom Cisneros worked as a White House Fellow in 1972.

"I hoped Henry would become a Republican when he worked for me. I thought he might have become one," said Richardson in an interview for this book. "Frankly, I had not become conscious he wasn't a Republican until I noticed his party identification in connection with the Kissinger Commission."

On many issues, Cisneros agrees with the pragmatic futurists such as Senator Gary Hart and Governor Richard Lamm. But he is uncomfortable with their style and rhetoric.

"Hart made too sharp a division between the party's past and its future. I don't like that," said Cisneros, who regularly quotes Franklin Roosevelt when he discusses his own new ideas and whose City Hall office has a photograph of John F. Kennedy hanging on the wall. In fact, Cisneros' favorite quote, which he uses in nearly every major speech, is a passage from one of Robert Kennedy's speeches:

"Our future may lie beyond our vision, but is not completely beyond our control. It is the shaping impulse

9

of America that it is neither fate nor chance nor the irreversible tides of history that determine our destiny as individuals or as a people. Rather, it is reason and it is principle, and it is the work of our own hands."

✓•   — The nationalization of Cisneros began in 1981 when at 33 he defeated a 58-year-old establishment businessman and became the first Mexican-American mayor of a major U.S. city and the youngest mayor in San Antonio's history.

In the 1981 mayor's race, Cisneros put together a coalition of Mexican-Americans, blacks, liberals, environmentalists, and conservative businessmen that not only won him the election but provided him a pluralistic mayoral base.

— San Antonio is a city famous for the Alamo, a tiny Franciscan mission where Texans were massacred by Mexicans in 1836. More than 10 million tourists visit the Alamo every year. It is a popular symbol of strength and patriotism, but the symbolism cuts two ways in San Antonio, the largest city in the U.S. with a majority Mexican-American population.

The battle of the Alamo was over in 1836, but San Antonio, situated 200 miles from the Mexican border and geographically closer to San Salvador than to Boston, is a city still negotiating between two cultures. The election of Cisneros—the consummate mediator—as mayor eased deeply-rooted bicultural tensions.

—San Antonio began as a Spanish military fort on the frontier. In 1690, fifty Spanish soldiers led by Don Domingo Teran de los Rios erected a cross at the headwaters of a river and christened the area San Antonio, in honor of St. Anthony of Padua. During the period when Mexico tried to free itself of Spanish rule, San Antonio became a battleground.

One of the major downtown streets, Dolorosa, got its name in 1813 when a Spanish force wiped out a Mexican rebel army and imprisoned 300 citizens. The captive women were forced to make tortillas for the Spanish army and were so mistreated that they named their place of imprisonment Dolorosa—the Street of Sorrow.

After the Texas Revolution in 1836, Anglo-Americans became the dominant culture. Cotton, cattle, and oil, the three economic staples of Texas, became the major sources of San Antonio's livelihood as well. After the Civil War, the city flourished and became a cattle capital when horses and cattle roamed through a winding area of downtown that early settlers described as a "skillet of snakes." The population grew so rapidly that until the late 1920's, San Antonio was the largest city in Texas, before Dallas and Houston surpassed it.

The downtown streets twist and turn like the river that travels fifteen miles beneath six miles of city blocks. Legend has it that the Indians who first settled on the river called it by an Indian name which meant "drunken-old-man-going-home-at-night." In 1939, then-Mayor Maury Maverick convinced his friend, President Roosevelt, to provide a Work Projects Administration grant to beautify the river. Since then, the river has been a major tourist attraction.

In the late 1960's, the city pulled together to sponsor a world's fair, "HemisFair '68," on approximately 100 acres in the center city. Though a financial failure, HemisFair attracted talented outsiders to San Antonio, many of whom stayed on after the fair to help wrestle political control of the city out of the hands of a business-oriented establishment.

San Antonio's urban political history followed a pattern similar to other Sunbelt cities. The 1940's saw the rise and fall of flamboyant municipal reformers; the fifties and early sixties were decades of sleepy efficiency when city government was in the hands of a few businessmen, and the late sixties and early seventies saw previously dormant interest groups demand power.

11

"What the population distribution means is that the cultures have to understand each other. And that is what is happening. This is a city that has had to learn to accommodate different points of view," Cisneros said after winning the mayor's race with 30-to-1 margins in Hispanic precincts and with impressive margins in Anglo areas.

Between 1981 and 1984, every major news organization in the U.S. traveled to San Antonio to tell the story of the urban affairs professor who vowed that economic development, not social welfare programs, would bring San Antonio out of the wilderness of an average per capita income of $5,672.

Pretty soon, it was difficult to separate the man from the city. In November 1982, he told *Forbes* magazine that as mayor he had something to prove—"That as a Hispanic, I would not run the city into bankruptcy." He added, "We're trying to prove that a Hispanic labor force is as capable, and has as strong a desire to learn and improve their lives, as any other people in this country."

Cisneros took every out-of-town reporter and camera crew who came to town on a drive through the West Side of San Antonio, pointing out new improvements—a drainage project here, new streets there—and describing his vision for San Antonio's future.

At some point during the tour, Cisneros would stop at a small Mexican-food restaurant and walk through the crowd of patrons, each of whom would greet the mayor by his first name. He would then introduce the reporter to the owner of the restaurant. After a taco or two, Cisneros and the reporter would be on a first-name basis.

After *Sixty Minutes* came to town and did a story on him, the nationalization of Henry Cisneros was complete. He became a national player without a trial by fire. He was only a two-term mayor of the third largest city in Texas. He'd never marched with Martin Luther King, or spent a lot of time in the political trenches. Nonetheless, he was in the big leagues.

The *Sixty Minutes* segment aired on February 26, 1984. Almost immediately, Cisneros was inundated with mail and telephone calls from all over the country. The calls came from both Democratic and Republican politicians currying favor; the letters came from ordinary Americans smitten by his charisma.

One man from California wrote, "I've watched public figures for just about fifty years, worked hard for the Roosevelt and Kennedy administrations with whatever tools the average campaign worker is given, and have undergone the usual wariness that comes with age. I was thrilled to see a rising young political figure who not only wanted to help his country and his party, but had great intellectual ability to do so."

A city manager from Washington state wrote to say that he had long ago given up on the idea that "in time a leader will come." The viewer told Cisneros, "You have, tonight, reinforced a weary hope that such idealism should not be abandoned."

Thousands of Mexican-Americans wrote letters telling Cisneros how proud he made them of their culture. One young man asked Cisneros to send him a "plan of success." The young letter-writer said, "Seeing a Mexican-American with your position, style, grace and abilities really makes me feel good. As corny as it may sound, it is an inspiration to know some do make it."

When Mondale stood in his driveway and introduced Cisneros to the national press, one of the pieces of evidence he offered for proof of Cisneros' suitability was his appearance on *Sixty Minutes*. Mondale wasn't talking about the power of CBS or even the power of Cisneros' message. Instead, he was talking about the style of Cisneros. Call it charisma. Call it force of personality or pizazz. Call it whatever you want. But whatever it is, Cisneros has it.

"At this point in our history," Cisneros told the re-

13

porters in Mondale's driveway, "as important as the traditional qualifications for the vice presidency are the untraditional values I bring to the table."

This is a book about the grandson of an immigrant. It is not the old immigrant story, because the Cisneros' grandfather didn't cross into Old America on the East Coast. He forded the Rio Grande into the parched, dry land now known as the Sunbelt.

Eleven-month-old Henry Cisneros, on the day he had his first haircut.

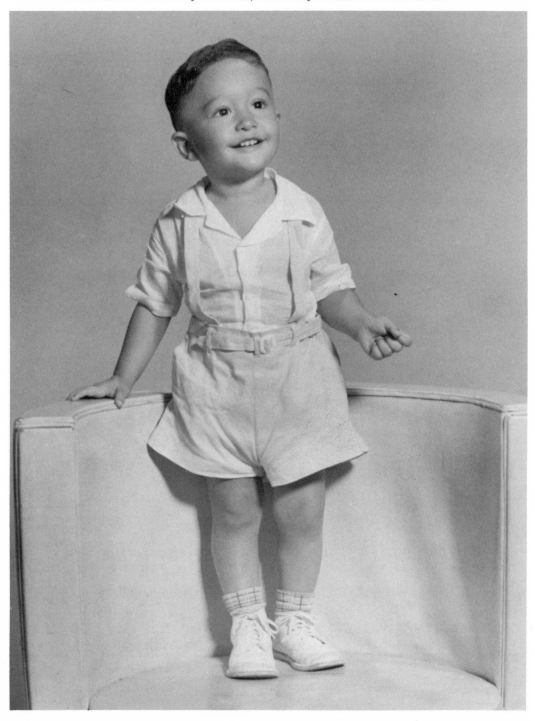

Romúlo Munguia, the grandfather of Henry Cisneros, who left Mexico in 1924.

Elvira Munguia at 18,
Jefferson High School Class
of '42.

George Cisneros at 21.

From left: George, Pauline, Henry, and Elvira Cisneros, when Henry was a preschooler and his father was a young military officer.

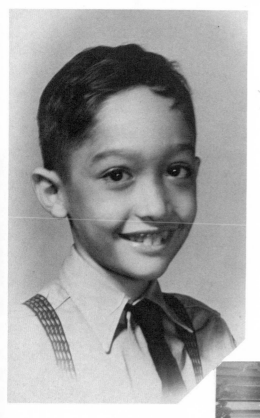

Henry as a kindergartner at Little Flower School on the West Side of San Antonio.

Henry and his sister Pauline ride a pony in the front yard of their parents' home on Monterey Street.

Pauline, 4, and Henry, 5, at a dance recital at
Woodlawn Gymnasium.

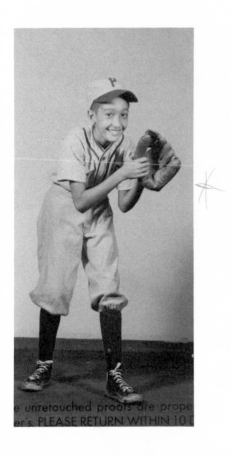

Henry, a ten-year-old Little Leaguer;
a freshman in the band at Central
Catholic High School; and (with bow
tie) in his senior class photo.

The whole Cisneros clan, from left: Pauline, Mrs. Cisneros, George, Jr., Tina, Col. Cisneros, Henry, and Tim. Below, at Texas A & M, Henry hits the dirt for a military drill.

In his senior year at A & M, Henry Cisneros became the first Mexican-
American ever to hold the position of commander of the combined
Aggie band. This was his graduation photograph, taken in 1968.

At A & M, Henry felt certain he wanted
to follow in his father's footsteps
and pursue a military career.

Some of his Aggie friends teased Henry
about having big ears.

Henry and Mary Alice Cisneros on their wedding day, June 1, 1969,
surrounded by family (and a mariachi band). Henry's grandfather,
Romulo Munguia, is seated at the head table, second from the
bride's left.

This family photo with firstborn daughter, Theresa, was taken in 1974, shortly after the couple returned to San Antonio from Harvard.

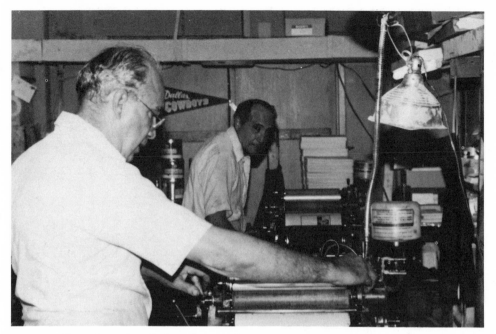

Henry's uncles, Ruben (left) and Romulo Munguia, at their printing business, where Henry and his brothers got their earliest exposure to the complexities of West Side politics.

Below: The mayor's brother George is shown working with a precinct group. (From left) Rose Garcia, campaign secretary; Fernando Centeno; Ben Walker, attorney.

Everyone in the family participates in the campaigns. The mayor-
elect's mother (left) and Tina, his sister (right), flank a happy
campaign worker on election night, 1981.

Below: On election night, 1981, an exhausted Tim Cisneros stands in a
crowded campaign headquarters as supporters await word of
his brother's election. (Photos by Catherine Cisneros)

"What now, Henry?" is a question that others ask even more often than the mayor himself.

II

North from Mexico

The story of Henry Gabriel Cisneros begins with the era of revolutionary tumult which engulfed Mexico from shortly after the turn of the century until the late 1920's.

The political persecutions, uprisings, and violent changes of government sent a flood of political refugees north across the Rio Grande. Few ever returned. Most stayed and carved out a new life in the Southwestern cities of the United States.

"I see Henry Cisneros," San Antonio historian Richard Santos has said, "as a product of the elite of the Mexican Revolution—of the political refugees and of their children who were the door-openers in the 1940's and 1950's."

The upheavals in Mexico brought a colorful succession of ex-presidents, generals, and high political figures streaming in and out of San Antonio. Arriving in 1926, near the end of the period, was Jose Romulo Munguia y Torres, the grandfather of the city's future mayor.

Years later, when Munguia had become a distinguished leader in San Antonio's large Hispanic commu-

1931

nity, few who did not know him well would have guessed that this frail and dignified intellectual had been deeply involved in the revolution.

6 Yet Munguia had lived through enough hair-raising adventures for several lifetimes before he came to San Antonio at the age of 41. Orphaned when he was eight, he found work as a printer's devil in Guadalajara.

7 Many years later, he wrote of his delight in the work of cleaning type, running errands, buying materials, and delivering completed jobs. By the time he was twelve he was working full-time and at fifteen he moved on to Mexico City as a skilled worker for an old family friend whose shop printed a famous newspaper, *El Hijo del Ahuizote*, for brothers who were radical opponents of the brutal regime of President Porfirio Diaz.

8 There he found himself caught up in the rising movement against the oppressive and corrupt rule of Diaz. The print shop was a center for the rising dissent. It printed open letters from activist leaders denouncing the plight of workers and peasants. Munguia and others were inspired to work without salary, realizing as they did that they were risking repression.

9 The political climate, Munguia later wrote, was one "in which it was truly dangerous to think, speak, and work for the restoration of the rights of the people which had been denied during the dictatorship. . . ."

10 One night in 1903, the inevitable police raid took place. Munguia and his fellow workers were among those arrested. He was jailed and sentenced to death—but later pardoned and released because of his age. He was only eighteen.

11 This was only his first brush with death. Twice more during the endless revolutionary campaigns in which he followed Venustiano Carranza, he was seized and sentenced to the firing squad, only to be rescued at the last minute. Once, a counterattack by friendly forces saved him. In another episode, he was given a cloak-and-dagger

assignment by the Carranza command to infiltrate the headquarters of a unit thought to be disloyal. Suddenly, loyal forces surprised the plotters, and, unaware of Munguia's mission, prepared to send him before a firing squad. Luckily, the military governor of Puebla arrived just in time to rescue him.

In later years Munguia described his role with Carranza's Constitutionalist forces as "an information officer" with responsibilities that extended into civil government. He was one of several highly skilled printers who published newspapers in areas under Carranza's control. A shortage of writers soon developed. Munguia, like many printers of the era, was a self-educated intellectual, and soon was writing his own vision of the principles of Constitutionalism.

One article dealing with the need to unionize women workers suggests ideas that were far ahead of their time. "The behavior of our female comrades need not be watched or judged," he wrote. "On the contrary, see the social evolution of the woman as a necessary thing, as a restitution of the freedoms and rights that for centuries have been selfishly denied her." Munguia busily organized workers into unions in areas in which he was publishing party newspapers, maintaining that to "organize is a right that the worker receives from nature as do all who populate the universe."

In 1915, when the Wilson administration recognized Carranza's victorious de facto government, Munguia was in Puebla where, among other things, he was publishing *Nueva Patria*, a newspaper devoted to the Constitutionalist cause. But he also soon became involved in enterprises which reflected his lifelong belief in the importance of education and his reverence for Mexico's cultural heritage.

He began a series of "Conciertos Civico-Populares" which included performances by the state orchestra, poetry readings, dancing, and, of course, patriotic speech-

17

es promoting government policies. Helping organize the events was a lively teacher from the orphanage, Carolina Malapica, a member of a prominent Puebla family. Soon Munguia was courting her and within a year they were married.

16 When the Constitutional Convention of 1917 met in Queretaro, Munguia was an alternate delegate and was able to take part as some of his own ideas were written into basic law. He viewed his selection as a delegate to be the "most significant reward of my life as a Constitutionalist, for with it, I have obtained the sanction of my revolutionary behavior."

17 Munguia's life was not to remain tranquil very long. When Carranza was overthrown and killed in 1920, he was forced out of his post as Director of Public Welfare in Puebla. He went back to the printing trade, but remained a staunch foe of the administration of General Alvaro Obregon. This led to his joining a revolt raised by Adolfo de la Huerta when Plutarco Elias Calles was designated by Obregon as his successor. The new revolution soon collapsed and Munguia found himself back in prison in Mexico City. Fortunately, friends were able to obtain his pardon and he returned to Puebla to establish a newspaper with his brother. But his standing with the government remained tenuous.

18 One night in January, 1926, six-year-old Ruben Munguia watched wide-eyed as his father prepared for a trip. He still recalls vividly how he and his older brother, Rafael, helped burn a mass of personal papers. In the morning his father left for San Antonio. "The day after that," Ruben Munguia recalls, "we were awakened by soldiers looking for him."

19 Romulo Munguia had a job waiting for him in San Antonio in the composing room of *La Prensa*, the leading Spanish-language newspaper in the Southwest at that time. Its staff was loaded with talented refugees from Mexico. Munguia's immense skill soon earned him the

18

post of mechanical superintendent of the thriving daily.*

20 Munguia arrived in Texas virtually penniless, but just two months later he was able to send for Carolina and the children—Rafael, Ruben, Elvira, and Guillermo.

21 As members of the middle class, Ruben has recalled, the Munguias were not exposed to the misery and humiliation encountered by thousands of other Mexican immigrants; nevertheless, his mother prepared carefully for crossing the border. She had been warned that all Mexican children had their hair doused with kerosene by U.S. officials who assumed they were infested with lice. "She took us to a barber shop in Puebla," Ruben remembers, "and had us shaved bald. She won her first battle even before she crossed the border."

22 The Munguias were part of a mass movement from Mexico that swelled the booming growth of San Antonio during the 1920's. In that decade, the population of the city's metropolitan area increased by nearly 50 percent, and Mexican immigrants accounted for a large part of the gain. By 1930, the census identified 98,000 people in the metropolitan area as "Mexican." They accounted for one-third of the residents of the city.

23 La Colonia Mexicana on San Antonio's West Side was a refuge, sometimes temporary, sometimes permanent, for dozens of revolutionary leaders, not to mention priests and even bishops of the Catholic Church. "The West Side," Ruben Munguia has written, "was a miniature Mexico City replete with all its intrigues, deals, plots, and counterplots and home of many exiled politicos, intellectuals, religious leaders, and a full array of army leaders, from generals to 'soldados razos.'"

---

*During this period, the administrator and editor of *La Prensa* was Leonidas Gonzalez whose son, Congressman Henry B. Gonzalez, represents a district that includes most of metropolitan San Antonio.

24 Visitors to the West Side found themselves immersed in the atmosphere of Mexico itself—women in black rebozos, vendors of candy and pan dulce, and countless shops selling herbs and potions of folk medicine. At dusk, portable chili stands appeared on Haymarket Plaza and their "chili queens" dispensed the fiery specialties of South Texas, while mariachi singers performed for patrons.

25 Life was not easy for Mexican immigrants, however. Pay scales were low, and soon to get lower with the onset of the Great Depression. In the Mexican-American slums, living conditions often were deplorable. Many families lived in "corrals" (pens), lines of huts opening on a common court, often with no running water. The miserable sanitary conditions led to periodic epidemics of infant diarrhea.

26 The West Side at the time was a center for the pecan-shelling industry and, during peak periods, as many as 12,000 workers were employed in it. A 1934 Labor Board hearing produced information that the average piece-work wage for a 54-hour week was $1.56. In the mid-thirties the city prohibited pecan shelling in the homes of workers and tightened sanitary regulations, but the exploitation of desperate workers continued.

27 Ruben Munguia remembers that his parents were offered a chance to operate a pecan-shelling business in the 1930's, but refused. "They didn't have the stomach to go into that kind of exploitation," he says. When workers finally resorted to a strike, Romulo Munguia offered them help and advice on organizing tactics.

28 Despite the difficulties facing immigrants who arrived on the eve of the Great Depression, the Munguias found the United States lived up to its promise as a land of opportunity. The boys went to work selling *The Saturday Evening Post, Colliers*, and *Liberty* throughout the downtown area. Their mother, meanwhile, made certain they were not skimping on their schooling. Her interest in

their education led her into a leadership role in the Parent-Teacher Association. Concerned over the many parents who were unable to participate because of the language barrier, she obtained permission from the Texas Congress of PTA to organize Spanish-speaking chapters in West Side schools.

29 The Munguia family quickly made its mark in San Antonio's "Colonia Mexicana." Within a few years Carolina Munguia launched a pioneer Spanish-language radio program on Station KONO—a lively mixture of conversation and music, featuring talented members of the community.

30 A year later, in 1932, she left the successful daily show when she became pregnant with her seventh child. Her husband left *La Prensa* and took over the program and it quickly began to reflect his fierce love of Mexico.

31 He emphasized Mexican music and culture and his commentary often dealt with the political situation south of the border. Meanwhile, with a small handpress earned by the boys in their magazine work, he began a back-porch printing operation. But it was a $300 purchase of ancient printing equipment that made the family business a full scale operation. With his background in the campaigns of the Mexican Revolution, Munguia must have taken special delight in one acquisition—an Italian-made cylinder press which had been used by Pancho Villa to print his revolutionary edicts and the currency to finance his operations.

32 The small print shop was an authentic family operation. Rafael was linotype operator and Ruben served as general manager and compositor. Guillermo was pressman and the youngest boys, Romulo, Jr., and Enrique were press feeders. Elvira immersed herself in the bookkeeping department and, when her brothers went off to military service during World War II, returned from her first year at the University of Texas to work on the Linotype and other mechanical operations.

33 Family members learned the value of work as children. "We all had to come in and clean out the composition boxes," recalls Elvira. "That's where we learned the ABC's."

34 In less than a decade, the shop had moved to larger quarters, had twenty full-time employees, and was printing not only the work of businessmen in the Hispanic community, but also virtually all the shopping circulars of San Antonio's independent grocery stores. Munguia Printers was on its way to becoming one of the city's largest printing operations.

35 Munguia, meanwhile, took his place as a leader of La Colonia Mexicana in San Antonio. The newly-emerging Mexican-American business community formed its own chamber of commerce in 1928 and Munguia became its secretary for eight consecutive terms. He devoted space to its community activities in a series of weekly newspapers he published during the 1930's and early 1940's.

36 Despite his successful transition to life in the United States, however, he never became a citizen. His deep love for his native country never wavered. He took a major role in celebrations of Mexican patriotic holidays in San Antonio, as well as in surrounding towns, and he immersed himself in efforts to develop cultural ties between San Antonio and Mexico.

37 This led to his early involvement when the University of Mexico experimented with annual extension courses in San Antonio, starting in the fall of 1944. Distinguished professors journeyed to San Antonio from Mexico City to teach language courses and lecture on Mexican archaeology, art, history, and literature. The yearly sessions were conceived not only to help preserve the heritage of the younger generation of Hispanics, but also to foster understanding and respect among Anglo-Americans— becoming a vehicle to counter prejudice in the majority community and encourage better relations between the United States and Mexico.

38 But by the early 1950's, the program faced serious problems of lack of support. Concerned San Antonians met in 1952 and formed an organization dedicated to maintain interest and support for the program—"El Patronato de los Cursos de Extension de UNAM." Munguia became its first president and led the organization for many years. The extension classes took root and grew to such an extent that the university established a permanent resident branch in San Antonio.

39 Just as it had cornered much of the printing of grocery circulars, the Munguia print shop became a headquarters for political printing. Partly for this reason, and partly because of Munguia's prestige in the Hispanic community, leading political figures sought his advice and support.

40 Munguia, however, was conscious of his Mexican citizenship, and it was Ruben who became the family's active participant in political campaigns, most notably in support of Maury Maverick, Sr., the colorful New Deal congressman who became mayor in 1939.

41 Romulo Munguia, Jr., vividly recalls an episode of his childhood when Vice President John Nance Garner sought advice on approaches to the Mexican-American vote. While his father met with the vice president in his Uvalde home, Mrs. Garner entertained Romulo and his sister with a tour of the house and grounds.

42 After he returned to the print shop from World War II service, Ruben became involved in the early efforts by young Mexican-American candidates to win county and legislative races, and in the presidential campaigns of Adlai Stevenson. He became an influential player in the intricate political games of the West Side and the shop became not only the place where politicians came for printing, but also for informal dialogue.

43 The senior Munguia, meanwhile, had long ago restored his ties to political leaders in Mexico. He played an active role in the presidential campaign of Miguel Aleman

23

in 1945. In a speech before the assembly of the ruling Partido Revolucionario Institucional (PRI) in Mexico City, he offered the endorsement for Aleman of an organization of Mexican citizens living abroad which he had founded.

44 During the closing stage of World War II, Ruben was stationed at Randolph Field at the fringe of the San Antonio metropolitan area. There he met George Cisneros who had been rotated back to the United States after spending 33 months in the Southwest Pacific and rising to be sergeant major of a combat infantry regiment.

45 One Sunday afternoon, Ruben drove a visiting family friend from Mexico to the air base to view the awesome B-29's stationed there. Elvira went along and Ruben brought Cisneros out of the barracks to meet her. "Let's go to the movies," Cisneros suggested, and he and Elvira proceeded to enjoy their first date, watching *Barbary Coast*.

46 There was nothing recent about the arrival of the Cisneros family in the Southwest. Its members were among early Spanish settlers in New Mexico, arriving nearly half a century before the American Revolution. There they lived on an old Spanish land grant and farmed and ranched for generations. But by the time the father of George Cisneros inherited his share, it was reduced to a long and rocky strip of land with little potential for a man seeking to rear twelve children alone after their mother died. When George started school at eight, he had his introduction to English. But most of his schooling was in Colorado where the family moved to work in the fields and where his father eventually was able to buy a small farm.

47 "From the time I was nine years old, I worked in the fields with my dad," George Cisneros reports. They followed the timetable of the sugar beet industry as migrants.
24 "In the spring," says Cisneros, "we had to drop out of

school nearly a month early to trim beets. It was stoop labor all day. In the fall we were a month late getting back to school because that is when you top the beets. I was always trying to catch up and sometimes it was Christmas before I did."

The youngsters went barefoot all summer to save their shoes for school. "My father would say that when we ran across the prairie, our feet were so hard that we would strike sparks if we hit a rock," he remembers.

Discrimination was pervasive. Cisneros never went into a barber shop when he was growing up in Brighton, Colorado. But despite the handicaps, he became one of the three Hispanic youngsters to graduate with his class from high school. He realized that education was his ticket to a better life and was prepared to "work twice as hard" as his classmates to achieve success.

His next step up the ladder was to a business school in Denver where he had gained a scholarship. There he got a good preparation for the U.S. Civil Service exam. He scored the region's highest grade and went to work for the Indian Service in Albuquerque and later Salt Lake City, before leaving for World War II.

After a six-month courtship, Cisneros proposed to Elvira, following punctilious Spanish customs demanded by her father. In the course of these preparations, he searched his original parish church in New Mexico for baptismal information and discovered that the family name was spelled with a capital "C" rather than with the "S" which he had been using. If he had not made the resulting correction, San Antonio's first Mexican-American mayor would have been Henry Sisneros!

Cisneros had no problem obtaining a civil service post in San Antonio, thanks to his prewar service and veteran's points. When his agency was shifted away from the city, he transferred to a civil service assignment in Fourth Army Headquarters in San Antonio's Fort Sam Houston, remaining when the Fourth Army was replaced   25 by Fifth Army Headquarters and climbing to successively higher assignments in the civil service and army reserves.

He was called to active duty as a lieutenant colonel between 1964 and 1968, but remained in essentially the same work at Fort Sam Houston. In 1968 he returned to civil service status while remaining active in the reserves. He was named chief of staff of the 90th Army Reserve Command and retired as a full colonel after suffering a stroke in 1976.

When George and Elvira Cisneros were married in 1945, they bought a home within a baseball throw of the original Munguia print shop. The crowded barrio was nearby, but there was no sign of it in the quiet neighborhood of modest frame homes. The area had originally been a center of San Antonio's German community, but the ethnic mix had become typically American. San Antonio's mayor of the period lived just a block away.

This was the neighborhood and family that greeted Henry Gabriel Cisneros when he was born June 11, 1947.

III

West Side Idyll

When Henry Cisneros reflects on the family and neighborhood in which he grew up in San Antonio, he evokes mental images of front covers of the old *Saturday Evening Post.*

"I guess my first recollections," he says, "are really twofold. One is of a personal family life and a neighborhood that was very wholesome and supportive. The other is of the larger family and my grandparents."

The neighborhood was in San Antonio's Prospect Hill section, an area of small but comfortable frame homes rising to the west of the city's core and its Mexican-American slums. To the young Cisneros, it was "a sort of Norman Rockwell" creation.

"There were sixteen boys my age in the block," he remembers. "It was just a matter of going out and hollering to get up a football or baseball game."

Still living along the tree-shaded blocks were older members of the city's large German community, but by the 1950's, it was filling up with middle-class Hispanic families.

"It was a very stable neighborhood," Cisneros said. "In fact, most of the families are still there."

Virtually all of the men worked in U.S. Civil Service jobs at Fort Sam Houston or at Kelly Air Force Base. Life was centered around church and families; neighbors were quick to help each other in times of illness or trouble, and they celebrated together at Christmas and New Year's. Fear of crime was non-existent.

Cisneros, now a university professor and mayor of San Antonio, has had a smorgasbord of choices of where to live with his wife, Mary Alice, and watch his two girls mature. He has remained within blocks of where he grew up—in the unostentatious frame home in which his grandfather, Romulo Munguia, lived until his death at 90 years of age.

One of his sharpest memories of childhood is of family gatherings at the Munguia home.

"Every Sunday we went there right after church," Cisneros recalls. "We would have lunch and an evening meal—or sometimes go on a picnic. I was very close to my Uncle Ruben and his kids."

The senior Munguia's commitment to passing the language and culture of his beloved Mexico to the younger generation was an important part of the family relationship.

"When I was ten or eleven," Cisneros recalls, "I would go and spend an afternoon at his house and he would leave a reading assignment in one of his books on Mexico for me."

The largely self-educated Munguia was a genuine intellectual and he had accumulated a large library on Mexican history and culture. As the president of El Patronato, he saw that his grandchildren were exposed to the visiting professors who came each year from the University of Mexico to teach extension courses.

"We would join him in greeting the professors at the airport," said Cisneros, "and on occasion we would attend lectures with him, though some of it was over my head."

Munguia was 65 when Cisneros was born. He was nearing 80 when he took his grandson with a group to Mexico City, where they climbed the pyramids and were immersed in the ancient city's history. Cisneros keenly felt his grandfather's total identification with Mexico and his "sense of public dedication."

"It was something rarified—not like the nitty-gritty of politics," he recalls, adding, "That's my Uncle Ruben's game."

Yet the basic formative influence on the first Mexican-American mayor of a major U.S. city was his close relationship with his parents and his four brothers and sisters.

The values of George and Elvira Cisneros were imprinted on their children from an early age. Their watchwords were hard work and education. George Cisneros provided a continuing example for his eldest child who recollects, "I'd come down for breakfast at 7:30 or 8 o'clock on Saturday and find he had already been working for two hours."

The senior Cisneros seemed always to be taking night courses at San Antonio College, or correspondence courses in connection with his army reserve duties, or to be making improvements to the family home. "He built a patio with his own hands," Henry Cisneros remembers. "He converted the upstairs attic into rooms for the boys. He added a room to the house. He was just incredible. Never did I see him lying around, drinking a beer."

In turn, strong-willed Elvira Cisneros was determined, in the words of her eldest child, "to be a formative force" in the lives of her sons and daughters. "She had the Munguia sense of destiny," he said, "of every person being somebody."

During summer vacation from school, Elvira Cisneros saw to it that all her children—Henry, Pauline, 29

CISNEROS

George, Jr., Tina, and Tim—were assigned specific household chores to perform during mornings. And she insisted that they stay home afternoons and entertain themselves in some creative fashion. Their friends were welcome to join them and often did.

Henry Cisneros became skilled at building model airplanes. He and his siblings sometimes wrote poems and stories. And, of course, he did a lot of reading. One summer he read 43 books.

George Cisneros encouraged the children to engage in lively discussions and they enthusiastically responded. Dinner was usually set for 5:30 P.M., but the family might not leave the table for hours. "Sometimes we'd still be there at 9 o'clock," Elvira Cisneros recalls.

Family visitors often were startled by the sheer intensity of the debates, but heated arguments were expected by George Cisneros. "I didn't want to inhibit them," he says.

Among his neighborhood friends, young Henry was always assumed to be the leader. The underlying reason was his sheer energy, combined with a rare ability for planning which he concentrated on childhood projects and strategies for games.

His plans were likely to be detailed and elaborate for even the simplest projects. His younger brother, George, Jr., recalls how preparations to play with model airplanes would call for several days of working in the dirt in the backyard while Henry meticulously shaped airport runways.

The Munguia print shop was only a few blocks away and Henry and George were frequent visitors. It was also a meeting place for a wide range of political figures who were having flyers printed or who were involved in campaigns with Ruben Munguia and Romulo, Jr. The boys heard discussions of political strategy and tactics and became expert in the design of effective campaign appeals.

30 George, Jr., recalls, "I would say, 'Wow, that's an interest-

ing flyer,' while Henry would be more into the philosophy involved in the issues."

They also heard firsthand accounts of the political dirty tricks that all too often swayed the course of campaigns in the Mexican-American barrio precincts. The brothers developed clear ideas of tactics that were morally unacceptable. But, as political opponents of Cisneros have discovered, they also learned the lessons of political hardball.

At the same time, they learned of the possibilities of working through the system, from their father's frequent participation on community committees working for improvements in city services. He demonstrated in action the family philosophy of facing problems and pragmatically solving them.

When it was time for Henry to begin his schooling, his parents enrolled him in the parochial school of the Church of the Little Flower. All of his brothers and sisters followed him there.*

When he entered school, young Henry had to accustom himself to speaking English rather than the fluent Spanish he had developed. He made the transition with ease. By the time he had completed the second grade, the sisters suggested to his parents that he skip the third grade, along with several other bright classmates. They felt he would be bored unless he were given a greater academic challenge.

The move was an academic success. Cisneros was forced to compete with older students and rose easily to the challenge. At the same time it had a downside. When he moved on to Central Catholic High School, it compli-

---

*All of the Cisneros siblings have pursued interesting careers. Pauline is a biologist; George is a composer and musician and retains strong political interests. Tim practices architecture in Paris; Tina is a journalist in Madison, Wisconsin.

cated his social life to be the only member of his group without a driver's license. But if development of his social skills was slowed a bit, he was on a fast track in more important areas.

At Central Catholic, the Brothers of Mary provided a strong academic program which attracted a rich ethnic mix of students from throughout the city. Many were from achievement-oriented Hispanic families like that of Cisneros himself. An impressive list of today's emerging Mexican-American leaders were at Central during that era. Among them were Ernie Cortes, whose work as a community organizer in Texas and California earned a MacArthur Foundation Award in 1984. And also William Velasquez, executive director of the Southwest Voter Registration Project, the driving force behind record registration of Hispanic voters in the Southwest in recent years.

"You got a good education with a kind of Christian social conscience to it," Cisneros has reported of his years at Central. More important, he met Brother Martin McMurtrey who became one of the key people in his educational development.

For Cisneros, McMurtrey was much more than an English and literature teacher. He was a motivator who transmitted his own excitement and belief in education to his students. He quickly sensed young Henry's unique talent for verbal expression and moved him into his most demanding section in English where his writing gained special recognition.

"It was the first time," Cisneros recalls, "that somebody said to me. 'You are right to play in this league and you are playing in the lead of this league.'"

Like other students at Central Catholic, Cisneros walked a few blocks from the campus on November 21, 1963, to see President John F. Kennedy's motorcade during his visit to San Antonio. It was a brilliant fall day and
32   the sight of the youthful president and his first lady riding

in an open limousine and waving to friendly crowds made a tremendous impression on the students. Cisneros was home from school in time to view a broadcast of the president's appearance at Brooks Air Force Base and hear him say that the United States had made an irrevocable decision to explore space and go to the moon.

The next afternoon one of the Irish brothers interrupted a class to announce to stunned students that the vigorous leader they had cheered only the day before had been assassinated in Dallas. Walking slowly home that afternoon, Cisneros composed a poem to express his feelings. It was later selected for an anthology of the best writing of San Antonio students. The poem closed:

> *The sky is gloomed with overcast.*
> *People stumbling along the streets cast eerie shadows.*
> *Through the murky, obscure dusk the flag*
>   *lowers to half-mast.*
> *Day is dark.*

Cisneros also excelled outside the classroom. He played French horn in the band and rose to executive officer in the school's crack ROTC unit. Stimulated by his love of aircraft and his father's career in the armed services, he was pointing toward the Air Force Academy and a career in aviation. It was not to be. He received only an alternate appointment to the Academy and was advised to spend a year at a military school and mature. After all, he was only sixteen years old and weighed only 135 pounds, even after a big meal.

The unaccustomed setback proved to be fortuitous. He followed the suggestion and enrolled at Texas A&M University and that changed the course of his life. Once he became an Aggie, he never turned back. "I got up there," said Cisneros, "and got elected to a class office and was named outstanding cadet in my unit and I got into the A&M swing of things."

33

The important thing about A&M was the rigorous challenges it posed, not just through its academic demands, but also through its Spartan traditions which molded the Corps of Cadets into a close-knit brotherhood. "At A&M," says Cisneros, "I learned what you can do when you go all-out. Most people don't really know what they can do because they operate within certain restraints."

Facing A&M's challenging environment, he decided that "not only was I going to survive, but I was going to perform in a competitive way." It was the right time and right place for such a resolution. "A&M in that era," Cisneros has argued, "was one of the last pure meritocracies left. If you could perform in the classroom, if your military performance was up to speed, if you had leadership capabilities, then there was no limit."

The skinny, jug-eared Mexican-American youngster who arrived in College Station from San Antonio's West Side in the fall of 1964 soon established himself as a competitor. He was chosen outstanding cadet in his unit in both his freshman and sophomore years, and outstanding cadet of his company at summer camp. At the close of his sophomore year he achieved a goal he had set for himself soon after he arrived in College Station. He was selected to be sergeant major of the Texas Aggie Band—the highest-ranking post that can be held by a junior in that elite organization. In his senior year he was named commander of the combined Aggie Band, one of the top leadership posts in the corps.

Early in 1967, an awed campus correspondent interviewed the sergeant major and detailed a long list of his activities. He was a member of the Ross Volunteers, the elite ceremonial honor guard of juniors and seniors chosen on the basis of leadership and performance, and held posts in four Memorial Student Center organizations concerned with planning a wide range of events. He was asked how he managed all the assignments along with his course work. "I just get things done that have to be done every day," he responded. "I set aside a certain amount of time for studying and then work around it." This meant that the hours he set aside for sleeping usually came to about five or six a night—a foretaste of his work schedule as mayor of San Antonio.

The most important lessons Cisneros learned at A&M, however, were not in the classroom or on the parade grounds, but in the Memorial Student Center which was directed by Wayne Stark, a legendary campus figure who had a knack for spotting students with special potential and helping them achieve it. "Wayne Stark," Cisneros says, "appeared to have made it his personal mission to make A&M a good experience for young Hispanics. He took young boys and basically shook them out of whatever lethargy they were in and sent them on to graduate school." Actually Stark's search for future leaders was not restricted to any ethnic or economic group, but was based on his perception of their latent potential. Today, "Stark's boys" make up an impressive network of successful executives in every part of the United States. Even so, a surprising number of Hispanic leaders in Texas laugh about being members of the "A&M Memorial Student Center Wayne Stark Mexican-American Mafia."

Stark spotted special potential in Cisneros which wasn't being realized. "I scolded him," Stark has recalled. "I told him, 'I've checked on some of your grades and they're not tops. '" (Henry, in fact, had been forced to repeat a course in calculus—a new experience for him.) He went on to tell Cisneros that he had the capability of earning good grades even while being a leader of the Cadet Corps and taking part in MSC activities. He stressed the importance of achieving an academic record that would open the doors of graduate schools.

The lesson took. "I was amazed," said Stark of the results. "The next semester he knocked out all A's. Something motivated him and he began to get leadership jobs

CISNEROS

in the Center programs." By the end of his junior year, in fact, his leadership qualities were so universally recognized that he was chosen chairman of the school's summer leadership conference of outstanding students from all areas of campus life. The annual event for some 100 leaders was held at a camp in East Texas. "He put it together and did a superb job," said Stark.

Stark's influence went far beyond academic advice. "He said to me," Cisneros recalls, " 'Look, the world is a lot more than you could possibly know and there are a lot of things that you should know that you are ignorant about—like music and art . . . opera . . . other kinds of leadership . . . the good things of the world . . . the good things of life.' "

Soon Cisneros was wrapped up in the work of the MSC's Student Conference on National Affairs (SCONA) which sponsored outside speakers and student conferences. He was chosen to be its finance chairman and that, in turn, meant that he was visiting Houston's towering office buildings to raise funds for the SCONA programs. Dressed in his trim uniform, he made his pitch to presidents of petroleum corporations and pipeline companies.

"We raised about $20,000 in Houston," Cisneros says. "I literally had to call on the chairmen of Shell and Pennzoil and people like that and sit down in their offices and explain how we needed money for the conference." It was an exciting assignment for the eighteen-year-old Mexican-American from San Antonio's West Side. Not surprisingly, a number of the executives he met were part of Stark's network of old Aggies. They responded not simply with contributions, but took Cisneros home to dinner or for an evening at the theater.

Such experiences were all part of Stark's strategy. "I want you to see how people eat and how people dress and how people live," he told Cisneros. "These are things you need to know." Now, as mayor of San Antonio, Cisneros has found his role reversed. "Stark is still doing it," he reported. "He'll write me a letter and say, 'I have a young man coming to town and I want you to see him....'"

Ultimately, it was through the broadening experiences of MSC that Cisneros developed a new vision of his goals in life—shifting his aspirations from military service to the demanding field of urban government. The change was precipitated during his junior year when he was chosen to take part in the Conference on United States Affairs at West Point, attended by student leaders from throughout the country. The experience was humbling. "I was totally outclassed," said Cisneros. "We sat around a conference table and I never opened my mouth. I was afraid to for fear that someone would ask me to follow up on my remarks."

The conference was loaded with students from elite universities. The mayor still chuckles when he recalls how he went up to one elegant Ivy League participant and asked how he managed to stay abreast of such a wide range of issues. "It's no problem," was the response. "I read the *New York Times* from cover to cover every day."

Cisneros didn't, of course, have access to the *Times*, and, besides, he was more likely to be polishing his brass and shining his Aggie shoes in the morning than reading a newspaper.

From West Point he went on to New York City for several days and found himself excited at "being in the city of John Lindsay, a mayor who had developed a reputation of walking the streets ... and realizing that, despite the fact that other urban centers were in disarray, New York seemed at least to be holding its own." That weekend as he flew home to Texas he read a *Time* magazine cover story on Daniel Patrick Moynihan and the urban crisis in America. The whole experience caused him to review his goals.

"My whole personal orientation," Cisneros said, "had been the MacArthur-like concepts of duty and honor and country. In fact, my dad had MacArthur's West Point

37

speech framed on the wall. I found it was possible for me to transfer those concepts to the domestic situation." That would mean spending his time on seeking solutions to the problems of the cities and to the related problems of restoring America's competitive strength in the world economy. He began taking local government courses and found that the idea of a career in the field "really made a lot of sense to me."

In the years since he left College Station, Cisneros, like most Aggies, has kept close ties with the school. He has served on several advisory groups for the university and has helped in recent efforts by A&M officials to increase Hispanic enrollment.

Graduating students were divided into three com- mencement ceremonies at A&M in 1984 and Cisneros was chosen as a speaker along with Vice President George Bush and Governor Mark White. The San Antonio mayor spoke to degree candidates from the Graduate College and to graduating seniors of the colleges of Agriculture, Geosciences, and Liberal Arts.

He touched on fond memories of his years in the Corps of Cadets, and of the influence of Wayne Stark and others on his development. "I have said on a number of occasions," Cisneros told the graduates, "that probably the most formative years of my life—that really changed me and put me on a course—were my years here at Texas A&M."

Henry Cisneros at 23, selected to be a White House Fellow during the administration of President Richard Nixon. (White House photo)

During his two years in Washington, Cisneros found himself working
with leaders of both parties, here with Senator Edmund Muskie.
(White House photo)

Cisneros was fortunate as a White House Fellow to join the staff of HEW Secretary Elliot Richardson, who strongly influenced his approach to public service. (White House photo)

Good people make good government work.

"This is not a time for complacency. It is a time to thrust for our full potential as individuals and as a people. This being done, there shall be no excuses necessary for the generations that follow."

Endorsed by
- AFL-CIO COPE
- Bexar County Women's Political Caucus
- SAN ANTONIO LIGHT
- National Association of Letter Carriers Branch 421

Cisneros
Place 3

Councilman Cisneros was one of the original leaders of United San Antonio, a broad-based group which generated approaches to the city's needs. He is shown above with Gen. Robert McDermott and Dr. Jose San Martin, his co-chairmen. (*Express-News* photo by Steve Krauss)

After winning a council seat in a citywide election in 1975, Cisneros faced a lesser challenge in 1977 when the council was elected by districts. The leaflet at left was produced in the Munguia print shop.

A 1977 meeting of the San Antonio City Council. Mayor Lila Cockrell is at the center, under the city's coat of arms. Councilman Cisneros (left) and Councilman John Steen (right), his 1981 opponent for mayor, sit next to the mayor. (*Express-News* photo)

As a councilman, Henry Cisneros worked closely with three-term Mayor Lila Cockrell and was considered her heir-apparent. (*Express-News* photo)

With members of his family beside him, Cisneros completes the process of filing for mayor in the City Clerk's office. (*Express-News* photo by Joe Barrera, Jr.)

A natural campaigner in any setting, Cisneros presses the flesh
with visitors to the Alamo. (Photo by Catherine Cisneros)

Below, the mayor makes his way through a blizzard of *cascarones*
at his 1983 birthday party. (*Express-News* photo by
Steve Krauss)

The jubilant mayor-elect rides in a San
Antonio Fiesta parade with Mary Alice
and their daughters, crammed into his
campaign Volkswagen.

Flanked by his parents, Cisneros takes the oath as mayor pro-tem in
1980. (*Express-News* photos by Steve Krauss)

Long-time staffer Barbie Hernandez goes over the 1981 vote canvass
with the mayor-elect. Below: a glimpse of the mayor in his role
as professor of urban studies. (*Express-News* photos by Jose Barrera,
top, and Peter Halpern, below)

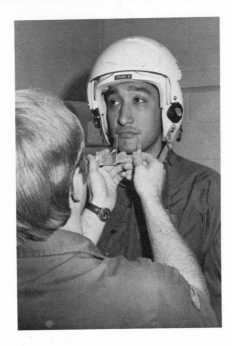

The Air Force is a major presence and employer in San Antonio. Cisneros buckles up for a test flight. (USAF photo)

The mayor rides with San Antonio police officer Alex Huizar. (Photo by Steve Krauss)

The mayor has placed special emphasis on recreation opportunities for youngsters. Here he is with Pop Warner League players. (*Express-News* photo by Trigg Gardner)

The whole family saw Cisneros off at the airport when he was named one of ten Outstanding Young Men by the U.S. Jaycees. (*Express-News* photo by Jose Barrera)

IV

Aggie Goes East

In 1966, when Henry Cisneros was a skinny, short-haired junior at Texas A&M University, Congress passed legislation establishing the Model Cities program.

Since it was up to President Lyndon Johnson to decide which cities received Model Cities funding, it was no surprise that San Antonio, located sixty miles south of Johnson's Texas Hill Country birthplace, was one of the 150 cities targeted for urban revitalization.

Cisneros' neighborhood was singled out for assistance. The office for the Model Cities Department was located two blocks from Sacred Heart Catholic Church, his home parish, and directly across the street from the Munguia family print shop.

"I had a chance to pick him up after he finished his work at Texas A&M and I jumped at it," said Roy Montez, director of the Model Cities Department in 1968. Montez later became director of the city's Department of Human Resources and now, in his thirty-second year as a public employee, he works as a trouble-shooter for the public works department.

"Henry first came aboard as an analyst but it was clear to me after a few months that he was smart enough to run the whole operation so that's what I let him do," said Montez.

[In January 1969, Cisneros, then only 21, became assistant director of the Model Cities Department in San Antonio.]Much of his time was spent negotiating differences between rock-ribbed conservatives at City Hall, who resented the federal government's intrusion, and angry West Side residents anxious to air complaints.

Under the Office of Economic Opportunity doctrine of "maximum feasible participation," anti-poverty programs were required to include the poor in the decision-making process. In some cities, such as Philadelphia, the Model Cities program did not significantly disrupt the balance of power. Often the war on poverty was waged by token representatives of the poor who had strong ties to the existing political structure. In other places, the practice of "maximum feasible participation" touched off race and class wars.

In Syracuse, New York, Saul Alinsky, a community organizer, encouraged students to "rub raw the wounds of discontent." In response to Alinsky's remarks, the mayor of Syracuse said, "We are experiencing a class struggle in the tradition of Karl Marx and I don't like it."

In San Francisco, a teenage leader of a black street gang was named administrator of a Community Action Agency program in response to citizens who argued "let the bad dudes run the program." The leader of a cultural enrichment program in San Francisco advised, "When you steal from the white man, you are dealing with real politics."

In San Antonio, residents who lived in the Model Neighborhood Area were organized into citizen councils. Complaints about lack of city funding of streets, drainage, and libraries were made public in heated hearings that lasted late into the night. Conditions in public housing projects were deplored. In the fall of 1969, angry residents marched on City Hall to protest the construction of a multi-family public housing project in the poorest school district in San Antonio.

"We had a 31-member board of directors which took up most of my time," Montez recalls. "Poverty-stricken Mexican-American housewives sat side-by-side on the board with established businessmen. Everybody had an equal vote so you can imagine the tensions. I was glad to have Henry to lean on. He virtually ran the office, which left me free to deal with the board."

It was during this period that the Good Government League (GGL), a business-oriented organization which had dominated local politics for fifteen years, began to lose its grip on the West Side. In 1961, before the Model Cities program galvanized the West Side into an effective voting bloc, Mayor Walter McAllister, the GGL incarnate, received 51.9 percent of the votes in what later became the Model Neighborhood Area. By 1969, McAllister's support had dwindled to 19.9 percent.

More significantly, GGL opposition candidates were scoring big wins. In 1969, Pete Torres, a feisty local attorney, won an at-large election to the City Council by running against the GGL. In the Model Cities area, Torres received 77.6 percent of the vote, even though his opponent, Alfred Vasquez, was a respected businessman both in the West Side and throughout the city.

"Everything I know about citizen participation and the mechanics of making government work, I learned during those Model Cities years," says Cisneros. "I'm a hands-on guy. I have to be in a situation, feel it, smell it, before I can understand it. I learned during those years that government is wise to put its money in physical projects—drainage projects, schools, swimming pools— because only physical projects leave a lasting legacy."

But the legacy of San Antonio's Model Cities program is as much political as it is physical. The issues that the

CISNEROS

Model Cities residents staked out in the late 1960's were the same ones that Communities Organized for Public Service built upon in the mid 1970's. They were also the issues that Henry Cisneros campaigned on in 1975 when he first ran for the City Council on the GGL ticket.

In 1969, running for political office was still a far off, distant dream for Cisneros. He had his hands full with the Model Cities program. Besides, that was the year he married Mary Alice Perez, his high school sweetheart.

Mary Alice's family owned a small grocery store in the same general neighborhood where Henry grew up. They first met at a baseball game when he was fourteen and she was twelve. "I remember she always struck out every time she was up to bat," Cisneros recalls.

For her part, Mary Alice remembers the game differently. "I don't remember striking out," Mary Alice told us, adding, "I do remember I was a team player and Henry was out to win."

The first clear memory she has of Henry was at a school fashion show at Sacred Heart Middle School. She was in the eighth grade. "I was modeling a brown and blue wool outfit," she says. "What I remember most was that Henry had big ears and not very much hair. I thought he was sort of ugly."

Both of them had parents who were socially strict. The youngsters didn't start dating until Cisneros was sixteen and a senior at Central Catholic High School. By then, Mary Alice was a sophomore at Providence High, an all-girls school located near Central in downtown San Antonio.

"We went to football dances and church events but we always went in groups with one or two other couples," Mary Alice remembers. "Henry was younger than other boys his age because he had skipped a grade. He didn't have his driver's license, so we group dated."

Henry went off to Texas A&M and Mary Alice stayed
in San Antonio, first finishing high school and then

taking courses at San Antonio College. In his senior year, they decided to marry but the wedding was postponed when Cisneros received a full scholarship from the Texas Municipal League to do graduate work. He stayed one more year at College Station and earned a master's degree in urban and regional planning while working as an administrative assistant to the city manager of Bryan, Texas.

On June 1, 1969, Henry and Mary Alice were married in a traditional ceremony at St. Agnes Catholic Church. They moved into a small garage apartment on Magnolia Avenue. Life was busy but fairly ordinary. Mary Alice had a job in the international department of Frost Bank. Henry worked long hours at the Model Cities job but, in retrospect, they had what seems like a luxurious amount of time to spend together.

They played cards with friends and went on a few camping trips. On weekends, they went to outdoor barbecues at Henry's parents' house on Monterey Street. They played touch football with family and friends.

"Even in those early days, Henry worked long and hard," Mary Alice says. "I learned to be independent enough to keep busy myself so that I wouldn't be just waiting for him to come home all the time."

While working in the Model Cities program, Cisneros came to the conclusion that the fundamental problems of poverty and joblessness on the West Side were not going to be solved by planners and bureaucrats. Well-trained and well-intentioned politicians would have to force a change.

"I decided I didn't want to work as a guy way down at the end of the process where you design physical things," Cisneros said. "I wanted to learn finance, budget, and taxes. I decided what I needed was not a degree in planning but a degree in administration and finance."

He applied and was accepted into the doctoral pro- 43

gram at George Washington University in metropolitan urban administration with an emphasis on finance. By January 1970, Mary Alice and Henry had packed all their earthly possessions into a Volkswagen Karmann Ghia and the two of them struck out for Washington, D.C.

Montez remembers Cisneros' last day of work in the Model Cities Department. "The staff got together and bought a cake that was shaped like a White House. The cake said 'Henry C. to D.C.' and there were lots of jokes about Henry running for president in 1992."

Today, Montez believes those jokes might have been prophetic. "At the rate Henry's going, he might make it to the White House before 1992," he says.

Henry and Mary Alice arrived in Washington, D.C., cold: neither of them had a job lined up and they didn't have any place to live. Mary Alice had never been away from home before, and was understandably anxious. So was Henry.

They stayed with Carmella and David Connally, friends of Henry's family, until they rented a tiny efficiency apartment on 16th Street, eight blocks north of the White House.

On a wintry Friday afternoon, Cisneros started out in search of a job. He went to see Allen Pritchard, the No. 2 man at the National League of Cities, whom he had met briefly in San Antonio at a Model Cities conference.

"When I showed up in his office, Mr. Pritchard seemed embarrassed about having told me to call on him. He said that they just didn't have any job openings for student interns," Cisneros recalls. Nonetheless, Pritchard had various members of his staff interview Cisneros over the weekend.

Cisneros must have aced the interviews because the following Monday he got a telephone call from Pritchard, who said that while he still didn't have a part-time job to offer, he needed a full-time administrative assistant. Cisneros jumped at the chance.

44

"I remember trying to dissuade Henry from taking the job because I thought it would be just too much with a full doctoral load, but he was determined he could do it," Pritchard recalls, then laughs out loud remembering his reservations. "I could not have been more wrong," he says. "I've never worked with anybody who used his time more effectively than Henry did. I came to rely on him totally because the quality of his work was so high."

Cisneros could not have chosen a better apprenticeship than the National League of Cities. In 1970-71, the first drafts of the revenue-sharing bills were written in the NLC office. Cisneros studied the programs and styles of many big cities mayors, such as Boston's Kevin White and New York's John Lindsay. It was while he worked at the NLC that Cisneros decided what he wanted more than anything in the world was to become mayor of San Antonio.

"He always used to talk to me about going home to San Antonio and finding a way to make economic development work," Pritchard says. "I remember he spent lots of time talking to folks at the D.C. economic development office. He knew that everything he learned about breaking the poverty cycle would be helpful to him in the future."

Soon after they settled in, Mary Alice landed a job in the international department of the Riggs National Bank, where she did translations from Spanish to English and clerical work.

She became pregnant. Two weeks before the baby was due, while Henry was in Florida at an NLC conference, their first daughter, Theresa, was born. Luckily, Henry's younger brother George was a student at Georgetown University and living with them at the time. George was watching a television special on the Apollo space program when Mary Alice told him she thought the baby was coming.

"When the first pains came about 2 A.M., I told George I thought we'd better go to the hospital. I'll never forget it because that night there was a terrible snowstorm," Mary Alice says. "I was pretty scared because the roads were icy and we skated our way to the hospital. But we made it and Theresa was born at 8 a.m."

In spring 1971, after the birth of his daughter, Cisneros was finishing the "routine, drudge work" of his doctoral courses in statistics, public finance, and administration. "Even though I was convinced I didn't have a prayer, I decided to apply for the White House Fellows program," Cisneros recalled.

The White House Fellows program was established by President Johnson in 1964 at the suggestion of Secretary of Health, Education, and Welfare John W. Gardner. [Every year, between fifteen and twenty people are selected as White House Fellows and assigned as assistants to members of the Cabinet or White House staff.] Competition for the fellowships is fierce; the year Cisneros applied, 3,000 others who thought they were the "best and the brightest" also applied.

George had misgivings about his brother going to work for the Nixon administration. However, Cisneros decided to apply for the fellowship anyway, despite his brother's misgivings and his own view that he didn't have much of a chance at getting it.

On paper, Cisneros did look like a long shot. According to the rules, applicants must be at least 23 and no older than 35. At 23, Cisneros was barely old enough to apply. For purposes of interviewing, the country is divided into ten regions. Cisneros was interviewed in Washington, D.C., which he thought would work against him because everywhere he looked in the nation's capital, he saw bright young people working in government.

"Actually, it worked in my favor," Cisneros said, "No Hispanic had ever come out of the Texas region. If I had interviewed in Dallas, I'm sure I would have been cut like all the other Mexican-Americans who'd interviewed before me. In Washington, at least I got a shot on the merits."

After his interview, Cisneros received a telegram telling him he was one of thirty finalists. The next step was a weekend-long competition at a Virginia resort.

"My mindset was that I was not going to make it. I looked around me that weekend and saw a guy who was No. 1 in his class at West Point, a Rhodes scholar, people who'd never lost any competition in their lives. I tell you the truth: I panicked."

He must not have panicked too badly, because, despite squaring off with University of Chicago economist Milton Friedman in one interview session, Cisneros was one of the sixteen selected for the fellowship in 1971.

He left his job at NLC and hitched his wagon to Elliot Richardson, who later became known as the Mr. Clean of the Nixon administration. Gene Dewey, executive director of the White House Fellows program, encouraged Cisneros to list Richardson, who was Secretary of Health, Education, and Welfare, as his first choice for a supervisor.

Cisneros went to see Richardson at HEW. "We really hit it off. I liked the way he was wrestling with the problem of HEW delivery of services in urban areas. I liked his style—Richardson is precise, calm, elegant, urbane. I was in awe of him," said Cisneros.

Still, Cisneros was worried that if he took the job at HEW he would be pegged as a "social-service type minority and I didn't want that." He pressed to work for Vice President Spiro Agnew but was assigned to Richardson.

"When I think of all the guys that went to jail in that administration and I wound up with Richardson, I can scarcely believe my luck," Cisneros said.

His relationship with Richardson was like the one he had with Stark at A&M. If Stark taught Cisneros to believe in the meritocracy, Richardson showed Cisneros there was a place for intellectual elites in politics.

"Richardson took an interest in me he didn't need to," says Cisneros. "He really went the extra mile for me. He would invite Mary Alice and me to social events. If they had four tickets to a play, they would invite us to go along. When I look back at what I wore to those events, I shudder. God Almighty, I didn't know how to dress."

To his horror, Cisneros remembers wearing a blue and white striped shirt with a gray and white striped suit to go to dinner with the Richardsons. "Not only did I not know you don't wear stripes on stripes, I thought the secret to good dressing was color coordination, so I often wore a green shirt with a green suit and topped it off with a green tie," he says. "Finally, I caught on and just started copying the way Richardson dressed."

Years later, when Cisneros was mayor, many out-of-town newspaper reporters came to San Antonio expecting to find Pancho Villa or Emiliano Zapata running City Hall. Instead, what they found was Cisneros in button-down starched Oxford shirts and dark business suits, looking like a Yankee blueblood. Little did they know he had fashioned himself in the aristocratic image of Richardson.

When we asked Richardson why he took the time and energy to be intellectual and political mentor to Cisneros, he told us: "Well, Henry was then and he still is an extremely attractive human being. I had never met someone from his ethnic group and background who had more potential. It wasn't only that he had a clear analytic grasp of policy issues that impressed me. I was attracted to his genuineness."

Richardson recalled that Cisneros wrote a memo for him describing in detail the most efficient, effective ways that HEW could deliver services to urban areas. "I still remember that memo because it was a clear exposition of the facts, but more than that Henry demonstrated an unusual ability to communicate public policy issues in human terms," said Richardson, thirteen years after Cisneros worked for him.

Cisneros says his most cherished moments with
48 Richardson were when he accompanied his mentor on

out-of-town trips and the two of them would have time to talk on airplanes. Typically, Richardson would carry two briefcases of work on board and tell Cisneros to draft his speech. It was pretty heady stuff for a 24-year-old from urban South Texas.

"I did it to the best of my ability, but sometimes I'd really blow it," Cisneros recalls. Once, Cisneros began a speech to a civil rights group with a quote from George Washington Carver. Laughing at his own naivete, Cisneros says, "Richardson threw it back to me and told me he wasn't the world's greatest devotee of Carver. He asked me to find something a little more contemporary."

Often, the two talked politics. According to Cisneros, Richardson taught him at least two political lessons that have stayed with him ever since.

Lesson No. 1 had to do with developing and protecting a political base. "One time we were on an airplane and Richardson told me to go back home to San Antonio. He told me that I couldn't be anybody in Washington unless I was from somewhere else and had a base. Young starry-eyed yuppies miss that. They go to Washington and get stuck in law firms. I try never to take my eyes off my base."

Lesson No. 2 had to do with how to survive in politics over the long haul. "Richardson told me the secret was to not scheme, or plan, or vie for the next position you want. Just do a very good job on the one you're doing now and the future will take care of itself. Richardson's own career looked like a diagram of upward mobility but he'd never even had in mind the next position. In effect, what he told me was there are few enough people who do a good job that the population narrows quickly when they start looking around for good people. Besides, if you don't do a good job, you've taken yourself out of the play anyway."

Near the end of their year together when Cisneros was about to leave for further graduate work at Harvard, Richardson wanted to make it clear to Cisneros that he had too much potential to waste it. During another plane

49

trip, Richardson predicted a struggle in the Democratic Party between liberals and conservatives. He thought minorities would be ideologically split, and told Cisneros that he would play a major role in the struggle. "You will be a national asset," Richardson told him.

Asked about the prophetic remark, Richardson says, "I wanted to be sure he understood his capacity. I didn't think he was the sort of person who would be made uptight by that kind of observation, and I thought it might strengthen his motivation."

Richardson was both right and wrong: His high expectations made Cisneros uneasy, but also steeled his resolve.

After Cisneros and the other White House Fellows returned from trips to Africa and Asia, he asked for and received $10,000 from the Ford Foundation to go to Harvard. "Mary Alice didn't like that first year at Harvard. She didn't work and we lived in a house with a hippie in the basement. She was cooped up with a baby on her hands and far away from home. I wasn't sure I could convince her to stay another year," said Cisneros.

He earned a second master's degree in public administration at the John F. Kennedy School of Government. In the summer, Cisneros went to Fort Benning, Georgia, for reserve training and Mary Alice spent some time in San Antonio visiting family and friends.

"Mary Alice really didn't want to go back to Cambridge, but we moved to a nicer apartment and put Teresa in a day care facility so she could find a job. It was a much happier time for all of us," said Cisneros.

The second year he worked as a teaching assistant at the Massachusetts Institute of Technology and completed doctoral classes. He finished the course work for a doctorate from M.I.T. but didn't write a dissertation because he was three-quarters of the way through the one he wrote for George Washington University.

50

"It's one of the great regrets of my life that I didn't go

ahead and finish the doctorate at M.I.T," Cisneros said. But Mary Alice told us, "I thought it was about time for the student to go out and get a job."

So he turned down a full-time teaching job at M.I.T. and accepted an assistant professorship at the University of Texas at San Antonio. In August, 1974, he and Mary Alice loaded up the Karmann Ghia one more time and headed southward, towards home.

V

Home to Politics

When Henry Cisneros returned to San Antonio in 1974, the city was in chaos. The Good Government League, the conservative political organization which had run the city for twenty years, was in shambles. The Anglo business establishment was divided into two warring factions. City government was paralyzed. Ethnic tensions ran high as Mexican-Americans made a long-overdue but painful drive for power.

Into this atmosphere of confrontation came highly educated Cisneros, respected by Mexican-Americans and not frightening to Anglos. At precisely the time the Anglo establishment realized it could no longer ignore Mexican-Americans, Cisneros arrived on the scene, willing to be courted.

In 1973, the GGL lost the mayor's race for the first time in its twenty-year history. Sensing the organization's demise, GGL leaders reached out in desperation to new bases of power. Cisneros' uncle, Ruben Munguia, lobbied behind-the-scenes to get his nephew on the GGL ticket. John Steen, a socially prominent businessman who later ran against Cisneros for mayor, chaired the nominating committee's secret deliberations. Helen Dutmer, a bold, aggressive South Side businesswoman, suggested Cisneros be placed on the ticket.

"There were some members of the committee who were opposed to Cisneros because after he was interviewed, they thought he was too liberal," recalls Dutmer, now a member of the City Council. "I knew the GGL was looking for a Mexican-American candidate and I just thought he was too personable and good-looking a candidate to pass up."

As a graduate student at George Washington University, Cisneros had written a paper examining the pattern of opposition to GGL candidates among Mexican-American voters. He concluded that anti-GGL feelings ran so high that Anglo independents historically had received more support than Spanish-surnamed candidates who ran on the GGL ticket in predominantly Mexican-American precincts. Given that pattern, why did he accept the GGL's nomination in 1974?

"It was more an act of self-confidence than anything else," Cisneros told us. "One way or another, I knew I'd make it come out alright. I didn't know in what role I would be cast but I was absolutely certain it would not be the traditional role of the Hispanic councilman on the GGL council. If I had to break with them, I would. If I had to cajole them into change, I would. But one way or another, I had no worry that I was going to be co-opted."

Still, he was willing to hold his tongue when other, less ambitious Mexican-Americans wouldn't have been able to control their anger. For instance, during a meeting in Steen's downtown office, Cisneros was asked by the GGL nominating committee if the fact that he was Catholic would put him in the position of having to take orders from the archbishop. It was the kind of insensitive question that could have caused Cisneros to explode.

"It was a 1950's-type question," Cisneros recalled.　53

"All I told them was that I owed no special allegiance to the archbishop. That seemed to satisfy them. Frankly, they seemed more interested in style sort of questions. They never did ask me to vote their way."

Once he became one of the nine members of the GGL ticket, Cisneros took charge of his own campaign with an energetic vengeance. San Antonio had never seen such a sophisticated media campaign. Everywhere he went, television crews followed. He held block parties in front of his parents' house and outdoor barbecues all over town.

"The same people who had given us wedding showers stepped forward to work on the campaign," Mary Alice recalls. "It was such an incredible grass-roots effort. Henry was writing press releases faster than I could type them and faster than any of us could deliver them to the papers." Mary Alice was pregnant during that campaign. One month after Cisneros was elected to the City Council, his second daughter, Mercedes Christina, was born.

GGL leaders didn't exactly know what to make of Cisneros' style of campaigning. They had raised $50,000 to pay for a unified advertising campaign for all nine candidates, and they criticized Cisneros for his free-wheeling tactics. He broke all the GGL's rules: He courted labor unions, refused to tell reporters to interview other GGL candidates, and campaigned eighteen hours a day on his own behalf.

When Cisneros dreamed up the idea of walking the entire length of the city in one day, GGL strategists were determined that he not get all the publicity. "All nine of the candidates decided to go," Cisneros says. "We started at Nogalitos and Zarzamora on the South Side on a coolish Saturday morning and walked all the way downtown to the Alamo. By the time the day was over, everybody was so sore they cussed me for two days."

On election day, twenty-seven-year-old Cisneros became the youngest councilman in the city's history and

the only GGL candidate to win without a runoff. Not even
Cisneros, however, broke the pattern of rigid opposition to
GGL candidates in predominantly Mexican-American
precincts. Cisneros won the election with 52 percent of the
vote. He received more votes among Anglos than he did
from Mexican-Americans. In fact, figures compiled by
Bob Brischetto, research director for the Southwest Voter
Registration and Education Project, show that in precincts where more than 70 percent of the voters were
Spanish surnamed, Cisneros received 44 percent of the
vote in 1975, which was double what other GGL candidates polled in those precincts but less than a majority.

For all practical purposes, the GGL was finished in
1973 when one of its own, Charles Becker, owner of a large
supermarket chain, broke rank and was elected mayor as
an independent. With Becker's election, a long-festering
feud erupted between the older, established business
community and the younger, risk-taking developers who
operated in the suburbs. In 1974, after Becker revealed the
city had been paying the Greater San Antonio Chamber
of Commerce roughly $1 million a year to attract new
industry to San Antonio, the suburban business establishment revolted and formed the rival Northside Chamber of Commerce.

Essentially, the business community was split be-
tween the remnants of the GGL gathered in the Greater
Chamber, located in the heart of downtown, and the anti-
GGL, surburban forces which held forth in the Northside
Chamber. In an effort to heal the split, the Economic
Development Foundation was formed in 1974 to recruit
new industry. The founder, Robert F. McDermott, a snowy-
haired retired general who is president of United Services
Automobile Association, worked hard to rally both cham-
bers around the unifying theme of economic development.
It was a Herculean task because feeling ran high in both
camps.

"The GGL crowd had tried to run me out of town,"   55 says Jim Dement, a North Side developer who was one of Becker's strongest backers. Dement moved to San Antonio from Dallas in 1963 and was appalled at the closed business society. "In those days, San Antonio was a little kingdom run by a small group of people who controlled all commerce and development. Becker opened up the doors down there at City Hall and told everybody to come on in."

Cisneros was one of only three GGL candidates elected in 1975. "By then," he recalls, "the structure of the GGL was so decrepit, so atrophied, so arthritic that basically the GGL sort of stumbled to the finish line and collapsed."

The death of the GGL didn't slow Cisneros down for a minute. He declared his independence as soon as he was sworn in on the City Council. Hardly a day passed that he didn't get prominent display in one of the two daily newspapers or the nightly television news. He seemed to be everywhere—braving angry German shepherd dogs to help read electric meters; riding with police officers, garbage collectors, fire fighters, and ambulance drivers; explaining complicated issues in nice coherent thirty-second segments for the TV cameras, and speaking to every civic club and neighborhood group in town.

"My inclination is to take the areas, the issues, one at a time, and learn everything there is to know about bonds, finance, housing, police and fire, public works, and drainage," Cisneros told James McCrory, veteran political reporter for the *Express-News* in early May 1975.

Many of the volatile political issues between 1975 and 1981 centered on growth questions. Would San Antonio grow in the same sprawling fashion that was the Sunbelt pattern in cities such as Los Angeles or Houston? Or would new industries be steered in the direction of older, inner-city neighborhoods where unemployed minorities were concentrated?

On most key issues, Cisneros favored directing growth back towards the central city. This put him at odds with

56

developers who were committed to suburban projects north of downtown beyond Loop 410, a belt highway around the metropolitan area.

If Cisneros had been forced to oppose the developers and new business establishment all by himself, he would have surely failed. But he didn't have to fight that fight alone. Fortunately for him, just at the time he was making his political debut Mexican-Americans were organizing at the neighborhood level to press for basic services in the older neighborhoods of the city.

In 1973, Ernie Cortes, another Aggie, came back home to San Antonio and set out to build Communities Organized for Public Service (COPS), a pressure group of more than 5,000 low to middle income Mexican-Americans that later became the most effective citizens organization in the nation.

[Cortes, a pudgy, intense man with angry, piercing eyes, graduated from Texas A&M University in 1963, five years after Cisneros. Both were ROTC members. Both were Mexican-Americans. Both were brilliant and disciplined. But they had fundamentally different ideas about how Mexican-Americans could best achieve political and economic power.]

[While Cisneros went the traditional role of electoral politics, Cortes took the road less traveled. When he worked with United Farm Workers President Cesar Chavez in Texas in the late 1960's, Cortes learned about Saul Alinsky's Industrial Areas Foundation in Chicago, where Chavez had trained in the 1950's.]The IAF's pragmatic style of working on issues that are of immediate importance to people's daily lives appealed to Cortes, who was by then disillusioned with the illusory nature of anti-poverty programs. After training at IAF headquarters, Cortes came home to San Antonio and started going from door to door on the West Side asking people what their problems were.

COPS members are not political radicals. Many work in civil service jobs for the federal government. Though the organization does not endorse political candidates and is staunchly non-partisan, its leaders can be generally categorized as Harry Truman-type Democrats. The organization is built around the parish structure of the Roman Catholic Church. From the beginning, church leaders nurtured and supported COPS. While individual COPS members were personally conservative, the Anglo business establishment was alarmed and terrified of the organization's confrontational style.

For example, to pressure the business community into supporting badly-needed drainage projects on the West Side, two hundred COPS members descended on San Antonio's largest bank and tied up bank tellers for hours by forcing them to change pennies for dollars. Tom Frost, board chairman of the bank, finally agreed to meet with COPS to hear their complaints about neglected neighborhoods. During the same time period, COPS members crowded into an upscale downtown department store and demanded service and courtesy from sales personnel as COPS rank-and-filers spent several hours trying on expensive clothes and buying nothing.

By the time Cisneros took his place on the City Council in 1975, COPS was an established political force in San Antonio whose leaders angrily challenged dominant institutions. COPS and Cisneros became allies on key issues, such as capital improvements for the West Side, the allocation of federal community development funds, and relief from ever-rising utility bills. But the organization kept its distance from Cisneros for fear of being co-opted, and Cisneros also kept his distance from COPS for similar reasons.

"I didn't know where COPS was going in the future. I didn't know what Ernie Cortes' agenda was, and so I gave them enough room to do their thing and I stuck to my own view of what was right," Cisneros recalls.

One of the first fights Cisneros led on the City Council involved a rate increase for Southwestern Bell Telephone Company. Instead of just opposing the increase outright, Cisneros stayed up all night preparing a complicated argument that the entire rate structure of the company should be redesigned because residents of the older parts of the city were subsidizing the installation of thousands of new telephones a year in the affluent northern suburbs. It was the first of Cisneros' many fights against urban sprawl and he won it.

"COPS would never admit it but I showed them with the telephone issue that they were missing the point by concentrating only on getting capital improvements," Cisneros said. "The major issue was that North Side development was being subsidized by poor people in the older neighborhoods."

On three significant issues during his first term on the City Council, the sometimes uneasy alliance between Cisneros and COPS proved mutually beneficial. Two of the issues involved natural resources—water and natural gas—and the third was a political fight over the method by which City Council members are elected.

The natural gas fight began long before Cisneros or COPS arrived on the scene. In June 1961, City Public Service (CPS), the municipally owned gas and electric company, signed a twenty-year contract with Alamo Gas Supply Company for natural gas delivery. Alamo Gas was a newly formed corporation owned by a small number of socially and financially prominent San Antonians. Before the ink was dry on the contract with CPS, Alamo Gas was swallowed up by Houston-based Coastal States Gas Corporation and its subsidiary, LoVaca Gathering Company.

In the unusually harsh winter of 1972-73, San Antonio discovered its twenty-year contract wasn't worth the paper it was written on. LoVaca didn't have anywhere

59

near the level of gas reserves it was supposed to have and couldn't meet its commitments to San Antonio's City Public Service. The city experienced brownouts as gas supplies were sharply curtailed. What's more, the contract price of about twenty-five cents per thousand cubic feet turned out to be a cruel joke. In the absence of reserves, LoVaca was having to buy gas in the OPEC-inflated market. In 1973, when the Texas Railroad Commission allowed LoVaca to pass through its higher costs to consumers, gas bills in San Antonio increased tenfold. Needless to say, tempers flared. Every Thursday when the City Council convened, hundreds of angry citizens crowded into the chambers, waving monthly fuel bills and demanding action.

In July 1974, CPS filed a $150 million lawsuit against Coastal States and LoVaca, claiming breach of contract. By the time other LoVaca customers filed similar lawsuits, the claims totaled $1.6 billion.

Almost immediately, lawyers for CPS and Coastal States started negotiating an out-of-court settlement. Cisneros kept the pressure up against such a settlement, which pleased COPS and won him enormous popularity all over the city. Headlines such as: "Cisneros: No Secret Deals;" "Cisneros Says Coastal Won't Keep Its Word;" "Shun Deals—Cisneros" put him firmly on the side of COPS, other hard-hit ratepayers, and a majority of the City Council led by Mayor Lila Cockrell.

"I was flying in the dark on the Coastal issue," Cisneros recalls. "All I knew was that an awful lot of people in town had been badly hurt by skyrocketing fuel bills. The establishment was knee deep in that thing, and I was determined to hold out for the best settlement we could get."

In any long-running controversy, there is usually one moment when tensions converge. In the Coastal States battle, that moment occurred in August 1976 during a particularly heated City Council hearing at McAllister

Auditorium on the proposed out-of-court settlement. As usual, various citizens' groups, including COPS, spoke against the settlement. Jim Dement, who had served on the mayor's blue-ribbon task force on energy matters, spoke in favor of the settlement, arguing that the $150 million lawsuit would only bankrupt LoVaca, leaving the city up the creek without a gas supplier.

Cisneros was furious at Dement's argument. In a long-winded, impassioned rebuttal Cisneros accused Dement of trying to steamroll the council into the settlement and ended by saying, "Mr. Dement, it's people like you who have had their boot on the neck of my people for generations." The crowd responded with a spontaneous and long ovation for Cisneros, but Dement left the auditorium angry and hurt.

Ironically, Dement later became one of Cisneros' major supporters in the 1981 mayor's race. "Nowadays, Henry and I laugh about that night," Dement told us recently, "but I'll tell you something; at that moment, Henry Cisneros was as close to leading a Raza Unida type revolt as I ever saw. My wife was in the audience and she was scared to death. I don't mind telling you I was scared myself."

Nonetheless, the momentum against settling was so strong that in December 1977 the Texas Railroad Commission ordered Coastal States and LoVaca to honor their pre-1973 contracts and refund the $1.6 billion to its customers. Everyone realized the Railroad Commission's order would mean certain bankruptcy for Coastal States and the settlement negotiations took on a more earnest, even desperate, tone.

One year and a half later, a settlement was finally approved. What San Antonio got out of the settlement was a stable supply of natural gas in the future from a newly-formed company, Valero Energy Corporation, headquartered in San Antonio, and some indirect financial benefit in the form of discounts below the market price of fuel. Coastal States escaped bankruptcy by getting free of $1.6 billion in customer claims.

One of the lawyers for CPS who negotiated the settlement plan defined a good settlement as one in which both parties believe they got the best of one another. By that definition, the city's settlement with Coastal States was a good one. One thing was certain: the resistance to a settlement from COPS, Mayor Cockrell, Cisneros, and others on the City Council forced Coastal States to make important concessions.

If the Coastal States battle did nothing else, it helped promote pluralism in San Antonio. Legal and political maneuvering was not confined to closed-door sessions. Confrontations took place in public.

The same high-pitched debate took place on the conflict over commercial development above the Edwards Aquifer, a huge underground reservoir that stretches more than 175 miles across six counties. The Edwards Aquifer is San Antonio's sole source of water. Environmentalists and consumers have long been concerned that uncontrolled development over the aquifer could lead to a polluted water supply.

Three months after taking his seat on the City Council, Cisneros came out publicly for stringent controls on development over the aquifer. "The basic consumer issue is going to be who pays and who benefits," Cisneros said at the time. "If the aquifer is allowed to become polluted, we will be asked to pay for treatment facilities and treatment of the water in our monthly bills."

At the height of the city's turmoil over growth policy, a majority of the City Council voted in October 1975 to allow construction of a large shopping mall on 129 acres over the area where surface streams recharge the Edwards Aquifer. COPS immediately announced its opposition to the super-mall. So did another citizens group, the Aquifer Protection Association (APA), an environmental group

62

which had organized earlier for the sole purpose of fighting to protect the purity of San Antonio's water.

Cisneros backed COPS and APA in their opposition to the council's decision on the super-mall. He supported the organizations' efforts to get enough petitions to hold a city-wide referendum on the issue. In December 1975, a referendum was held and by an overwhelming margin of 4-to-1 San Antonio voters rejected the super-mall. The mall's opponents, including Cisneros, had won a major victory.

In the wake of the mall referendum, COPS and APA called for a sweeping eighteen-month moratorium on construction over the Edwards' recharge zone. It was then that Cisneros made the beginning of his break with COPS. Cisneros couldn't bring himself to vote for the moratorium because he agreed with the city attorney that it was probably illegal. At the same time, he couldn't side with the developers. When the key vote on the moratorium was held in June 1977, the moratorium was adopted by a margin of 6-4. Cisneros abstained from the vote.

"That vote pained the hell out of me," Cisneros told us. "I left the council chamber after it was over and went back in the hall to a little restroom. I looked at myself in the mirror and I was pale. COPS was mad at me. The North Side developers were mad at me. I just couldn't win."

In January 1978, the Fourth Court of Civil Appeals of Texas reversed the moratorium. Cisneros was proven correct; the moratorium was illegal.

If his critical abstention on the aquifer moratorium was the beginning of his break with COPS, the real split came in March 1979 when COPS leaders called Cisneros a "traitor" for refusing to support a resolution that called for the city to stop contracting with developer H. B. Zachry until Zachry agreed to repair homes COPS leaders charged were shoddily constructed. Cisneros argued that while the homeowners had legitimate grievances, the city   63 should not impose "economic sanctions" against a major developer.

"It was a very decisive issue for me," Cisneros said recently. "With that vote, I established psychological distance from COPS."

While the battles over water and natural gas supplies were significant, no single event so fundamentally changed the face of San Antonio municipal politics as the change from an at-large, city-wide system of electing City Council members to a single-member districting system.

It all started in July 1976 when the U.S. Justice Department objected to massive annexations that had taken place in San Antonio from 1972 to 1974 on the grounds that the Anglos in the newly annexed areas diluted the voting strength of Mexican-Americans. The Justice Department offered San Antonio two choices: Either fight the ruling in court, or adopt a single-member districting system to provide more equitable representation of minorities.

There was strong opposition to following the federal government's fiat. Many San Antonians thought the Justice Department's contention was unfair. A local delegation went to Washington to lobby Texas Congressmen to initiate legislation to block the ruling. When all was said and done, Cisneros cast the deciding vote in opposition to going to court and in favor of changing the City Charter to allow for ten council districts with the mayor elected at large. Like COPS, he campaigned long and hard to adopt the change in the City Charter. The proposal received overwhelming support among Mexican-American voters and was narrowly approved with 52.7 percent of the vote.

The 1977 City Council election confirmed the worst fears of arch-conservative Anglos about districting: Mexican-Americans won five of the 10 district seats, and one black council member was elected as well. Ethnic

64

minorities wound up in control of 6 of the 11 votes on the council.

Cisneros won reelection with more than 92 percent of the vote. "I came in here as a novice and a greenhorn," Cisneros told his supporters on election night, "but I've learned the ropes and I can tell you one thing. In the next two years, I'm going to produce."

He was riding high, enjoying success on the issues and immense popularity. Then he suffered two crushing defeats back-to-back.

First, he lobbied to become mayor pro tem and the council rebuffed him in a heartbreaking 6-5 vote. He was especially disappointed that Mayor Cockrell had voted against him. Cisneros had withheld support for an old family friend, Dr. Jose San Martin, who opposed Mrs. Cockrell in the 1977 mayor's race. He felt Mrs. Cockrell owed him. He felt equally betrayed by Councilman Glen Hartman, with whom he had worked closely during the previous council term, but who decided to oppose him on the mayor pro tem bid.

Frustrated and angry, Cisneros drafted a letter of resignation from the City Council and gave it to a radio reporter who put the story on the air. The next day, Cisneros held a press conference on the front steps of City Hall and said that he was not resigning. "It's good to be taught a lesson," Cisneros told reporters that day, "good to be humble."

He was humbled again in 1978 when San Antonio voters overwhelmingly defeated a $98.4 million bond issue that Cisneros and the other five minority City Council members supported. COPS had also supported the bond issue but Mayor Cockrell and the four Anglo council members campaigned against the bond issue which primarily benefitted the south and west sides of the city. On election night, Mayor Cockrell said, "I feel the vote is a mandate to the council to close ranks and for all members to be concerned about the city as a whole, rather than their own districts."

Shortly after that, the six minority City Council members started to seek compromises. Ethnic tensions eased. In 1979, District 6 Councilman Rudy Ortiz was defeated by only 84 votes by Bob Thompson and the ethnic balance shifted back to the Anglos. That same year, COPS, which had earlier accused the Economic Development Foundation (EDF) of selling San Antonio as a cheap labor town, signed a peace treaty with EDF in which both parties agreed on broad economic development goals for the city.

Cisneros knuckled down to trying to attract new industries to San Antonio. In 1980, he led two expeditions to Minneapolis to woo one of the nation's premier high tech companies, Control Data, to San Antonio. Representatives of COPS, EDF, and Cisneros all sat around the same table at Control Data's headquarters and convinced Bill Norris, chairman of the board, to locate a plant in an inner-city neighborhood.

The era of defiant confrontation was past. COPS had won and lost enough fights to realize it was time to compromise. So had the business community. Cisneros was ready to make his move to become mayor.

VI

The Last Battle
of the Alamo

In September 1980, Henry Cisneros was jumpy, like a racehorse anxious for the sound of the starting gun but unable to find the gate.

Cisneros was chomping at the bit to run for mayor, but the time was not quite right. There were still too many unknowns, not the least of which was whether Mayor Cockrell would seek a fourth term.

In 1975, Mrs. Cockrell had become the first woman elected mayor of a city with a population over 750,000. Hers was a calm, gracious style of leadership. She had started out in politics as a volunteer for the League of Women Voters. The low-key leadership style she developed as a young housewife and mother working with the League stayed with her throughout a political career that spanned more than twenty years.

In the early 1960's, San Antonio's business establishment drafted her to run for the City Council on the GGL ticket. Once elected, Mrs. Cockrell quickly carved out for herself a consumer advocate's role.

By 1980, she had brought divided City Councils together through the change to the controversial single-member districting system, the stormy rise of Communities Organized for Public Service, and the long, bitter battle with the city's natural gas supplier.

During six years as mayor, Mrs. Cockrell never raised her voice, not even in November 1979 when she had police evict Councilman Bernardo Eureste from the council chambers because he refused to submit to her gavel and come to order.

As she contemplated seeking a fourth term, Mrs. Cockrell made it clear she wasn't the least bit tired of the job. When she was asked in October 1980 how she felt about being mayor, Mrs. Cockrell told reporters, "I just love it, love it, love it."

Such comments kept Cisneros awake nights.

"For months, Lila had given me hints that maybe she wasn't going to run, but she wouldn't tell me for sure," Cisneros recalls. "It nearly drove me crazy."

For instance, one day Mrs. Cockrell called Cisneros to her office at City Hall, like a queen summoning a prince-in-waiting. She advised him to get his outstanding travel vouchers into the city clerk's office, hinting lack of attention to such matters could prove publicly embarrassing to a mayoral candidate.

Mrs. Cockrell was torn between her own desire to run again and her husband's health problems. Sid Cockrell, who served as executive director of the Bexar County Medical Society for twenty-five years, suffered a mild heart attack in late 1980.

Since 1963, when his wife was first elected to the City Council, Cockrell had fulfilled the role of political spouse with dignity and patience. His health now figured heavily in Mrs. Cockrell's calculations about a possible fourth term.

"I'm still in the throes of a tough decision," Mrs. Cockrell told reporters in October 1980. "I thoroughly enjoy the role of mayor and I'm having many people urge me to run again. At the same time, I'm weighing the situation personally. My husband and I feel I have made a substantial contribution in time to the city and now we're reviewing our goals." She promised to announce her go-no-go decision after the November presidential election.

While she was trying to make up her mind, Cisneros was preparing to run. [In filing cabinets in his district office on West Commerce Street, Cisneros had on index cards the names of 90,000 San Antonians that he considered good bets to support him for mayor. He'd been collecting names since 1975 when he first ran for the City Council. The truth of the matter was that by 1981 Henry Cisneros had been running for mayor for six years.]

More important than the 90,000 names of supporters were a core group of about seventy volunteers who met every three or four weeks to help Cisneros define campaign themes. The "inside team" included family members such as his brother George who had come home from Houston to run the campaign, but also included old childhood friends, young lawyers, entrepreneurs, union leaders, and Democratic Party activists.

From the beginning, one of the tactical problems of the Cisneros campaign was organizing the army of volunteers who wanted to work. He insisted that everyone be given "meaningful work" to do, whether it was developing one of the issue papers, organizing a phone bank, or block walking. By the end of the campaign, he had six campaign headquarters operating in different quadrants of the city, plus a twenty-four-hour operation in a barnlike building downtown. It was George's job to tell people no, and the person he had to say no to the most often was his brother Henry.

"Henry just couldn't believe we were as organized as we were," George told us. "He'd come into the headquarters and start second guessing, and I'd have to tell Mary Alice to get him out of there so we could get some work done."

By October, the whole campaign was raring to go. Said Cisneros: "We had picked an announcement date for late November or early December, but Lila asked me not to go ahead with it because she felt it would put her in an awkward position. We were really at this decision: Either do it, damn the torpedos, no matter who the opponent is, or get out of politics."

By "we," Cisneros meant himself. He was frustrated by the jockeying and positioning that was going on, and felt he would lose his political edge if he had to serve a fourth term as a District 1 city councilman. "1981 was do or die for me," he told us.

He wasn't the only man in town who felt that way. John Thomas Steen, a three-term councilman and millionaire businessman, was feeling equally frustrated.

In 1977 and 1979, Steen had come very close to running for mayor. Both times, he decided against it because polls showed he had almost no chance of beating Mrs. Cockrell. In 1981, Steen decided to listen to himself instead of political pollsters. Like Cisneros, Steen was convinced 1981 was his now-or-never year.

After all, Steen had paid his dues. His life story read like a Horatio Alger saga. His family moved to San Antonio in 1929 from Yoakum, a small Texas town, when his father faced hard financial times. "We lived in ten or eleven houses when I was growing up," Steen told *Express-News* reporter Rick Casey during an interview in 1980. "My mother says my father would find a house where the rent was $3 cheaper and we'd move. But he did make sure to stay in the same area so I wouldn't have to change schools too often."

The elder Steen got a job as a bookkeeper in a San Antonio insurance firm. When one of the partners of the firm died, Steen's father bought his interest. Young Steen went off to Austin to study business at the University of Texas, where he graduated in 1943. He served as a naval officer during World War II, and saw combat in several battles including the D-Day invasion of Normandy. After the war, he returned to San Antonio and bought into his father's insurance business. When his father died, Steen poured time and energy into the business, guiding its rapid growth. By 1980, he wasn't just directing one insurance firm but three separate firms where about fifty independent agents sold life, fire, and automobile casualty insurance.

At 59, he had also spent an enormous amount of time on civil and social endeavors. He was past president of seventeen civic organizations and had presided over everything from Boy Scout meetings to the once-omnipotent GGL.

What's more, he was a card-carrying member of San Antonio's upper class. He was a member and officer in every private club in town—the San Antonio Country Club, the Argyle, the St. Anthony Club, and the Order of the Alamo. In 1967, he was crowned King Antonio for the Fiesta Week celebration, an honor highly coveted by established families but viewed by many Mexican-Amercans with derision as an oligarchical symbol.

In 1967, when Steen zoomed through the streets of San Antonio in an open-air convertible as King Antonio, it seemed like the right thing to do. In those days, San Antonio was a town ruled by a small group of businessmen who worked in downtown banks and law firms, played tennis, golf, and poker at the San Antonio Country Club, and were well-organized politically under the auspices of the GGL. Yes, it was elitist. Yes, GGL tickets were hand-picked by a small group. But until the turbulent 1970's, the majority of San Antonians were content to let a small group of elites rule by consensus. The GGL had, after all, made sweeping reforms in city administration and greatly improved city services. GGL administrations were clean and efficient. Between 1955 and 1973, the GGL had won 73 of the 81 council races. But times changed. New interest groups—COPS and a new group of developers and businessmen—elbowed their way up to the table and demanded their share of the pie.

Steen saw himself as a stable, solid businessman willing to work with diverse groups. He had supported the move to single-member districting in 1977, much to the displeasure of some of his old GGL colleagues. He had remained open to the idea of public housing projects in his districts. He was not, in short, a political Neanderthal.

When asked in early 1980 what kind of mayoral campaign he planned to run, Steen answered: "We're going to see John Steen as a successful businessman who can bring stability to the city, who knows finance, who has seen good times and bad times. We're going to see a leader who has been elected president of seventeen different organizations."

The problem was that Steen was the right candidate —genteel, sincere, accomplished—at the wrong time. If he had run in the heyday of the GGL, he would have been anointed mayor. The problem for Steen was that in 1981 neither the new business establishment nor COPS would sit still for a candidate who represented a past era. Steen conjured up images of Mayor Walter W. McAllister, patriarch of the GGL, who ran the city with no-nonsense efficiency in the 1960's. Two decades later, San Antonio was not at all sure it wanted another businessman mayor.

✦ Tensions between the old and the new ran high even before either Steen or Cisneros announced their candidacies. It was a foregone conclusion that Steen would receive support from the old-money crowd and from die-hard Republicans who were angered by Cisneros' endorsement of President Jimmy Carter. It was also clear Cisneros would receive support from COPS' constituencies, from young, upwardly mobile professionals, and hard-core Democrats. The unanswered question in the fall of 1980 was: Where would the new establishment developers and business people go?

"I had heard Lila was having meetings with the

business community and I was absolutely positive the purpose of these meetings was to indicate her uncertainty, only to have the businessmen shore her up and tell her she had to run," Cisneros told us.

During the same period, Cisneros was also meeting with business people, trying to persuade them to get on his bandwagon early because he had the momentum and organization to win, and asking them not to encourage Mrs. Cockrell to run. Among the monied group that were early supporters of Cisneros were former Councilman Cliff Morton, who had participated in the successful revolt against the GGL, and investor Dan Parman.

Parman, who grew up in Uvalde, had never been publicly active in San Antonio politics before the Cisneros campaign. In 1980, he announced a $1.5 billion, 15-year development past Loop 1604 in the far-flung northern suburbs of San Antonio. His investment in the city was considerable, and as the 1981 campaign approached, Parman was determined to protect it.

"I grew up in an area where Mexican-Americans had been held down and oppressed for years and years," Parman told us when we asked him why he decided to support Cisneros. "I saw what happened in Crystal City when the Mexican-Americans finally came to power. It was strictly confrontational. The confrontation had been building in San Antonio, and with Cisneros I saw a chance for peace. I liked what he was saying about economic development, and I guess I just believed that theory about a rising tide lifting all boats."

Parman remembers the day Cisneros came to his office and asked for a campaign contribution. "It was real early in the game. Henry didn't even have any stationery for the campaign yet," Parman said. "He asked me to help him raise $3,000. I remember thinking: 'I don't know anything about running a political campaign, but I sure know you need a heck of a lot more than $3,000.' "

Parman lined up the city's developers and new businessmen to support Cisneros. Typically, the businessmen whom Parman and Morton brought on board were members of the Northside Chamber of Commerce, which had been organized in opposition to the GGL-allied downtown chamber. They also weren't members of the San Antonio Country Club and none of them had ever been King Antonio. They had memberships in the new country clubs that had sprung up north of Loop 410. As one big-money investor put it at the time: "What this election is really about is the Oak Hills Country Club versus the San Antonio Country Club and us Oak Hills boys are going to beat the hell out of the old guys."

On December 8, 1980, Cisneros received a telephone call at home from Morton, who had just come from a meeting between the suburban business elite and Mrs. Cockrell. Morton told Cisneros that Mrs. Cockrell was going to announce the following day that she would not seek reelection. Morton wanted to meet with Cisneros before Mrs. Cockrell made the announcement.

"I had breakfast with him on the North Side," Cisneros told us, "and he wanted to know where I stood on a number of issues—water, energy, economic development." Over eggs and biscuits, Cisneros laid out his economic development program for Morton. When he was finished, Morton told him: "If you mean what you say, then we'll support you."

At that moment, San Antonio's new generation of private sector powerbrokers—men such as B. J. "Red" McCombs, Jim Dement, John Schaefer, Jim Uptmore, and Ray Ellison—totally switched over to Cisneros. Not only did they help Cisneros raise $247,000, but their support meant that Steen could not credibly portray Cisneros as anti-business. It also left Steen with only the old establishment as a base of financial support.

The next day, Mrs. Cockrell met briefly with both Cisneros and Steen in her office at City Hall and told them she would stay neutral. The public statement she made to reporters was simple: While she had "mixed emotions" about not running, she and Sid felt it was time to "devote more time to our personal lives."

Cisneros wasted no time in being the first to officially announce his candidacy in a press conference extravaganza at the Menger Hotel, located in the heart of downtown San Antonio adjacent to the Alamo. Television cameras photographed him standing in front of an ornate wall between an American flag and a Texas flag. The room was large enough to include his family and a large crowd of eager volunteers, but small enough that many people were forced to stand. He started out with a general statement of things that needed doing, but the central theme was economic development as a unifying force in San Antonio.

Five days later, Steen made his expected announcement, portraying himself as a mature businessman who would bring fiscal responsibility to City Hall. "Just as every family must take a hard look at their budgets and what they can realistically afford, the City of San Antonio must look at its budget," Steen told reporters. From the outset, Steen seemed self-conscious about his own lackluster style. At the opening press conference, he made an obvious reference to Cisneros' impressive media skills. In a rare catty moment, Steen said, "Some leadership is symbolic and charismatic, but real leadership is setting goals and providing sound direction."

At that point, the other critical unknown was whether another Mexican-American would jump in the race for mayor. Now that Cisneros had the support of a substantial group of Anglo businessmen, he began to fret over the other key ingredient to his campaign—the undivided loyalty of Mexican-American voters.

Eloy Centeno, rotund owner of a chain of supermarkets, was making noises about running against "Li'l Henry," as he patronizingly called Cisneros. Centeno saw himself, not Cisneros, as the first modern Mexican-American mayor of San Antonio. During the height of citizen unrest over skyrocketing fuel bills in 1975, Centeno, then a member of the board of trustees of City Public Service, was defeated in a mayoral bid. Among the more controversial planks in his platform was a proposal to establish a red-light district to control sex crimes.

Centeno made no secret of his mistrust of Cisneros. Part of it was generational jealousy—he simply believed ambitious young Cisneros had not yet paid his dues. He was also suspicious of Cisneros' relationship with Anglo businessmen.

"Eloy thought he was the logical person to be the first Hispanic mayor," Cisneros told us. "But there was also someone spiking him and that someone was Bill Elizondo."

Cisneros is convinced that Elizondo, an optometrist who later served a controversial stint as president of the board of trustees of San Antonio's inner-city school district, led a behind-the-scenes "Stop Cisneros" move among Mexican-American politicos. Elizondo denied he led such a move.

Cisneros believes two men—former State Senator Bob Vale and West Side produce magnate Frank "Pancho" Sepulveda—finally persuaded Centeno not to run in 1981.

"There was a meeting held with Eloy, which was supposed to be the meeting at which Elizondo pushed him into running," Cisneros told us. "Vale came out for me and told Eloy that he could not win. Another person who was in the room and said the same thing was Pancho Sepulveda."

If Centeno needed any further discouragement, the decision of Councilman Frank Wing and State Representative Frank Tejeda to support Cisneros was the final straw. Wing, Tejeda, and one of Centeno's top-level employees, Edmundo Zaragoza, were leaders of a South Side political organization that had produced reliable results at the polls. When Tejeda and Wing broke ranks with

Zaragoza to support Cisneros, Centeno threw in the towel.

Even though Centeno was out of the race, Hispanic opposition did emerge. Dr. Jose San Martin III, the namesake son of the man who introduced Cisneros to politics in 1975, announced for mayor near the end of the filing period. The San Martin family was still miffed at Cisneros for not supporting the elder San Martin's mayoral candidacy in 1977. Even though young San Martin was a political newcomer, Cisneros was worried about his entry into the race. The San Martin name was well-known and respected among Mexican-Americans. To make matters worse, U.S. Representative Henry B. Gonzalez' son, Henry B., Jr., signed on as San Martin's campaign manager. The congressman immediately disassociated himself from the San Martin candidacy and endorsed Cisneros.

San Martin's campaign never really took off, which led some Cisneros campaign workers to suspect that San Martin was never a serious candidate but was in the race as a spoiler to draw Mexican-American votes away from Cisneros. "We'd seen that divide-and-conquer tactic so many times on the West Side that we just had to be suspicious," George Cisneros told us recently. That suspicion was fueled in February 1981 when one of Steen's campaign workers, Tony Cortes, surfaced as San Martin's treasurer.

Dr. Tucker Gibson, a local pollster and Trinity University professor who worked for Steen in 1981, said the consensus inside the Steen camp was that while Centeno might have run strong enough to force a runoff between Steen and Cisneros, San Martin would not. "The San Martin candidacy was always a mystery to us. He never had any strength," Gibson recalled recently. Asked if San Martin was encouraged to run by Steen operatives, Gibson said: "I don't think San Martin had to be prompted." Ultimately, San Martin's candidacy was insignificant: He received less than one percent of the vote.

Steen was having problems of his own. Early in the campaign, pollsters for both Cisneros and Steen said Cisneros had a staggering lead over Steen. Steen's own polls showed he trailed Cisneros 27 percent to 47 percent. Cisneros' polls showed 50 percent of respondents supported him, while only 19 percent said they would vote for Steen.

Cisneros' polls were conducted by George Shipley, the leading Democratic pollster in Texas, who was the chief strategist for Cisneros in 1981. Normally, Shipley works for big bucks but he did the Cisneros campaign for peanuts because "quite frankly, I'd never seen any political candidate that had the amount of raw political talent that Cisneros has."

"Candidates win elections, not pollsters, and Henry Cisneros won that 1981 election lock-stock-and-barrel," Shipley said. In dog-and-pony shows with contributors, Shipley laid out the numbers which showed Cisneros was practically a shoo-in and suggested it was in their best interest to go with a winner. His polls showed ethnic tensions had eased and the mood of the community was optimistic and hopeful. At one of the meetings, someone raised the question about the electability of a minority candidate. One of the developers quipped, "Yes, I believe it's time we can elect an Aggie mayor."

At one point when Cisneros told Parman he needed still more money, Parman said he wasn't sure he could come up with any more. Cisneros launched into a speech about how important it was for him to win to bring peace to the warring factions of the city. Parman replied with a laugh, "Henry, I'm not sure how much more peace I can afford."

With polls showing Cisneros with an overwhelming lead and funding sources drying up all over town, Steen's campaign was floundering. Groping for direction, Steen brought in some big guns. He hired two out-of-town Republican political consulting firms to help raise his low profile and target his supporters. Nancy Brataas, a former state senator from Minnesota, was recruited to set up a phone bank operation. Brataas had helped engineer Republican Governor Bill Clements' upset victory in 1978 by mobilizing 16,000 volunteers in 35 phone banks. In addition, Steen hired Bailey-Deardourff, a Washington-based consulting firm that worked for Gerald Ford in 1976 and Ronald Reagan in 1980.

The strategy of Bailey-Deardourff was to portray Cisneros as erratic, immature, indecisive, and unreliable. In the final weeks of the campaign, Bailey-Deardourff convinced Steen to launch an attack on Cisneros' financial backers. On radio and television, Steen questioned the motivation of five prominent businessmen who contributed heavily to Cisneros.

The ads backfired badly. Four of the five businessmen who were named promptly told the press Steen had solicited contributions from them. Steen was not running a poor-boy campaign himself: In the end, he wound up spending roughly $13,000 more than Cisneros. Perhaps most important, the ads were not consistent with Steen's gentleman image. It was out of character for him to be negative.

"For the ads to have worked, John would have had to stay on the offensive," Tucker Gibson told us. "John was not prepared to run a really negative campaign. He's too nice a man to fight a gutter fight."

George Cisneros wasted no time in responding. Within a matter of hours, he had ads on the radio taking Steen to task for negative campaigning. "Shame on you, John Steen!" began the counter-ads. But Cisneros himself was hesitant about how to respond to the ads. A few weeks before the election, a long-faced Shipley told Cisneros that his lead had slipped dramatically since Steen started the negative ads.

Shipley told Cisneros that unless he took Steen on publicly for accusing him of selling out, then he might

79

just lose the election. Two days later, Cisneros struck back in a press conference at a downtown hotel. He attacked Steen for hiring out-of-town consultants to tell him what to do, and posed the question: If the businessmen who were supporting him were such bad men, then why had Steen asked them for contributions as well?

Steen's reaction was to blame his Washington-based consultants for the ads, and to suggest that if Cisneros couldn't take the heat, he ought to get out of the kitchen.

In the final weeks of the campaign, correspondents for all three networks, the *Washington Post*, the *New York Times*, *Newsweek*, *Time*, and *La Prensa* of Mexico City descended on San Antonio. Even then, Cisneros was being described as one of the new generation of post-World War II leaders likely to play an important national role in the future.

On election day, Pat Clayworth, the president of the San Antonio Teachers Council who ran Cisneros' phone bank operation, had volunteers manning 200 telephones. "We had about 40,000 identified supporters and I think Pat Clayworth called every single one of them on election day," Cisneros recalled. Cisneros himself jogged through the city all day long behind a sound truck, coaxing supporters to get out to vote.

• ⌈The hard work paid off. On April 4, 1981, an unexpected record number of 155,831 voters turned out at the polls. Cisneros received 61.8 percent of the vote, racking up huge margins in predominantly Mexican-American precincts and as much as 45 percent of the vote in Anglo areas. The most diverse coalition in the city's history had elected Cisneros the first Mexican-American mayor of a major U.S. city.⌋The word went out across the land: The Battle of the Alamo was finally over. San Antonio began a long honeymoon with Cisneros.

Fresh from victory in the 1981 mayoral race, Henry Cisneros is carried to a podium at campaign headquarters for a speech. (*Express-News* photo by J. B. Hazlett)

Children run to shake hands with Mayor Cisneros and his family during the 1984 Fiesta Flambeau parade. (*Express-News* photo by Charles Barksdale)

Cisneros speaks to members of Communities Organized for Public Service (COPS). Councilman Bernardo Eureste (far left) adjusts his tie. (*Express-News* photo by Jose Barrera)

Cisneros signing an autograph for Licha Fernandez at a 1983 political fund-raiser. (*Express-News* photo by Rick McFarland)

Cisneros drops by Immaculate Conception Church on the West Side to visit with Maria Tellez, precinct captain; Arturo Guajardo; and (right) Consuelo Garcia. (*Express-News* photo by Bob Owen)

Cisneros, the ultimate media-oriented politician, makes his way down the halls of the Bexar County courthouse as Shirl Thomas and Barbie Hernandez, trusty staff members, bring up the rear. (*Express-News* photo by Joe Barrera, Jr.)

The mayor in conversation with Archbishop Patrick Flores and
Rabbi Morley Feinstein. (*Express-News* photo by Jose Barrera)

All this and he sings, too, . . . here helping out a mariachi band at the
Arneson River Theater. (*Express-News* photo by Craig Stafford)

(*Express-News* photos by Steve Krauss)

With his own hands, Cisneros repairs a whopper chuckhole in downtown San Antonio. (*Express-News* photo by Robert McLeroy)

(*Express-News* photos by Steve Krauss and Peter Halpern)

Cisneros vowed to be an active mayor when he first ran in 1981. Here he is in 1984, picking up garbage on the South Side. (*Express-News* photo by Jose Barrera)

The mayor holds Dorothy Masterson on his lap, surrounded by other children on the front steps of City Hall. (*Express-News* photo by Joe Barrera, Jr.)

Cisneros opens his campaign headquarters on West Commerce Street in 1983. (*Express-News* photo by Peter Halpern)

Cisneros is shown here about to throw a ball at a dunking-booth at Rosedale Park. (*Express-News* photo by Charles Barksdale)

Left, struggling to maintain a nonpartisan posture, Cisneros introduces President Reagan at a 1983 Cinco de Mayo celebration. (*Express-News* photo by Scott Sines)

Three times a week, Cisneros makes time to run. Here he is running at night through San Antonio streets during a race held to celebrate the All-America City award in 1983. (*Express-News* photo by Peter Halpern)

Republican Governor Bill Clements (left), Cisneros, and County Judge (now U.S. Representative) Albert Bustamante (right) unveil a monument recognizing the contributions of Hispanics. (*Express-News* photo by Charles Barksdale)

Cisneros shows off St. Paul's Square, a downtown redevelopment project, to (from left) Dr. Stanley Green, president of the Laredo Heritage Fund; Elmer Buckley, special assistant to the mayor of Laredo; L. A. Guerra, member of the Webb County Commissioner's Court; and Al Cervera, vice president of Avante Corp. (*Express-News* photo by Charles Barksdale)

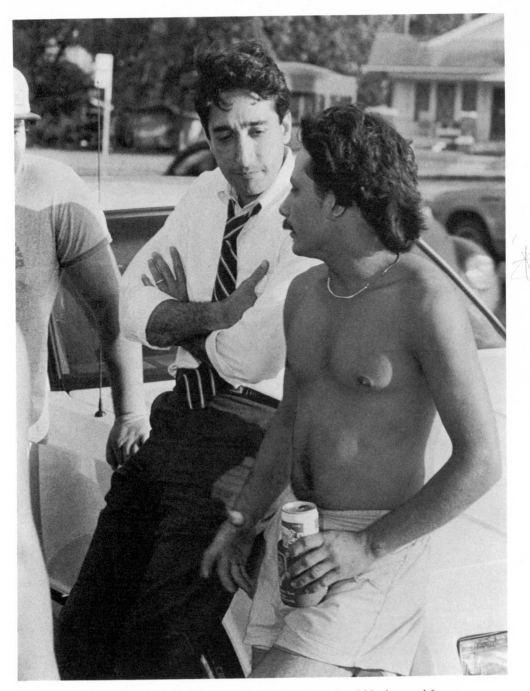

During a 1984 controversy about whether beer should be banned from public parks, Cisneros talks with a resident of the Woodlawn Lake area. Eventually, a ban was put into effect in some parks. (*Express-News* photo by Charles Barksdale)

With a statue of Mexican independence hero Father Hidalgo in the
background, Mayor Cisneros addresses a crowd gathered to
mark Mexico's Independence Day, September 16, 1983. (*Express-News*
photo)

VII

Feeding the Grass Roots

San Antonio reached a critical turning point in its ⤴ long history as Henry Cisneros took office as mayor on May 1, 1981. His election marked the final decisive shift in the city's political power base reflecting the emerging Mexican-American majority.

The change came at a time when the turbulent political battles of the 1970's, in which Chicano activists challenged the stand-pat conservatism of the establishment, were still fresh in the memory of most San Antonians. The 1977 charter referendum which broadened representation on the council had been adopted by a margin of only 1,673 votes out of a total of 61,387 cast.

The election of a Mexican-American mayor could have been followed by a dangerous polarization of politics. Instead, Cisneros served as a bridge between the Anglo ⤝ and Hispanic communities and his greatest service to the city may prove to have been his success in developing a strong new sense of community unity.

Midway through the mayor's second term, George Shipley, the Texas political consultant who has been

closely associated with Cisneros, reviewed his performance. "He has been able to unite the different interests in
San Antonio as never before and to reach out and involve
diverse factions within the community on critical tasks,"
he said. "The immediate benefits of that have been a
sense of community purpose and pride."

Taking a longer view, Shipley argued that Cisneros
"has been able to point the community in some very
positive directions which will equip it to survive and grow.
I know of no other city in recent years which has har-
nessed so many government resources behind economic
development."

The city's political consensus was demonstrated in
down-to-earth fashion in the passage by a 5-1 margin of a
$61 million drainage bond issue which was the first phase
of a giant program to solve the city's storm flooding problems—a festering issue in the Hispanic neighborhoods
for many years.

In the same election in April 1983, San Antonio
voters placed an unprecedented stamp of approval on
Cisneros, reelecting him with 94.2 percent of the vote.

The job of mayor in San Antonio was designed by the
framers of the 1951 council-manager charter to be largely
ceremonial. The charter gives the mayor no real power.
Other than providing that he is to receive $3,000 in addi-
tion to the annual council compensation of $1,040, it
scarcely differentiates between the mayor and other
council members. The very restricted remuneration for
council service has, of course, greatly restricted the field
of contestants for office—especially for the job of mayor.
For most of his first two terms Cisneros had no option but
to shoulder his back-breaking responsibilities and ex-
hausting schedule for no recompense at all—state law
would not allow him to receive payments from the city
while he was at the University of Texas at San Antonio,
even though he was teaching a reduced schedule at com-

parably reduced pay. Starting in January 1985, this legal roadblock was removed when the mayor joined the faculty of Trinity University as a visiting professor of urban studies and became free to draw payments from the city.

In addition to his University of Texas salary, Cisneros had been receiving fees for speaking appearances and his total income in 1983 was estimated to be in the $50,000 range. In addition, Mary Alice Cisneros holds an executive-level promotional job with a San Antonio-based photo finishing firm.

Trinity, with an endowment of $150 million, has been engaged in a serious program to become one of the nation's leading small liberal arts institutions and has been paying top salaries to academic stars. It is assumed on campus that Cisneros probably will receive a salary comparable to or better than the $43,000-a-year average for full professors. This will enable him to slow his furious pace of speaking engagements.

It was not until after the election of Mayor Lila Cockrell in 1975 that a mayor became a full-time presence at City Hall and the role of the mayor began to expand beyond traditional patterns and into the realm of economic development. During her three terms, the city began to assume an aggressive role in generating jobs in cooperation with the private sector through Urban Development Action Grants. A department of economic development and employment was launched at City Hall, though the move caused unease in conservative business quarters.

Cisneros swiftly expanded these initiatives into a whole new dimension. The change in the role of the mayor, he has explained, was inevitable. "It's a national phenomenon," he says. "What was once the traditional role of city government—to pick up the garbage, to make sure there are enough police on the streets, to fix the potholes—has gradually evolved into a more expansive role. In the 1950's and 60's, cities began to be concerned about overall

83

development planning and so major downtown revitalization became a front-burner agenda in cities such as Boston and New Haven where the earliest use of urban renewal for major downtown revitalization occurred."

The evolution was speeded by Lyndon Johnson's Great Society projects in the mid-1960's. "We saw cities beginning to have to address the whole agenda of social problems," recalled Cisneros. "Cities became the recipients of federal grants to do everything from neighborhood gang prevention to adult education to rodent control, and the human resources departments came into existence on a large scale."

Concern with human resources led inexorably to concern about jobs and economic development—something Cisneros absorbed firsthand during his experience in San Antonio Model Cities program. "You could see very dramatically," he says, "that simply spending money in a social services strategy to deal with symptoms, but not going to the root cause of poverty and low income and high unemployment rates, was not going to be a long-term solution for cities. So today one of the dominant themes of city governments across the country is the theme of economic development."

Mayors now must face a transition in their role. "They are beginning to explore," says Cisneros, "the issues associated with technological change. It's the vocabulary of venture capital, research parks, higher education cooperation for technology. . . . It's what I refer to as the new infrastructure of economic development. The old infrastructure was that associated with ports and roadways and iron ore and coal and waterborne transportation. The new infrastructure is this sort of thing."

The changes in San Antonio's political scene during the late 1970's prepared the way for the sort of active and aggressive role in economic development which has been pursued by Cisneros. Not only did the shift to district representation and the simultaneous surge of minority political influence play a part, but there was also a change in attitude in the broader community.

"What had previously been a city that had been satisfied to be provincial and on the sidelines," commented Cisneros, "has become a city that has forcefully chosen to be aggressive."

Economic development is particularly important to San Antonio. Unquestionably the city has a strategic location within the Sunbelt and in recent years has been routinely included in lists of cities for which strong and healthy growth is predicted. Yet as recently as the 1980 census, the San Antonio metropolitan area ranked behind the state as a whole in median family income and per capita income, and was much higher than the state average in the percentage of its people living below the poverty level.

The 20th Congressional District which covers the heart of the city has remained one of the poorest in the nation. The 1980 census showed that 20 percent of its families were below the poverty level. Needless to say, the burden of poverty falls most heavily on the city's large minority population. This has given a special urgency to the efforts of city government to improve the economic base.

A mayor cannot dodge his economic responsibilities, Cisneros believes, "First off," he explains, "just as the president gets blamed or praised with respect to the national economy, so too, prosperity of the city—the whole question of whether the city is prospering in a general sense—is something the mayor has to [consider]."

Cisneros is concerned with more than statistical abstractions when measuring this. "There are many ways to interpret what you call prosperity," he says, "but my definition of it is that everyone has access to the economic benefits of our society."

This means that a city's leaders must "consciously work at increasing opportunity." That, in turn, requires

"a generally prosperous and healthy economy overall."
This, he argues, is a "precondition for economic progress
for minorities." Emphasizing his point, he asserts: "Anybody who believes it can be done without an overall climate of prosperity—that minorities can make progress
without that—is mistaken because it is a precondition."

A major theme for Cisneros in his approach to his role
is summed up in one word: inclusiveness. That requires
"making sure everyone is at the table," and also calls for
"giving everyone a stake by involving everyone—not just
in the decision-making, but in the creation of the community ethic." Such an inclusive process eliminates potential
roadblocks to community action, Cisneros argues.

Without question, San Antonio has been able to
broaden grass roots participation in decision-making in
recent years. "I think we've successfully transformed the
ethic in San Antonio," says the mayor, "from a city where
it is generally acknowledged that decisions were made at
the Country Club by a handful, to a community where
there are multiple power centers and in which successful
policy is the outcome of negotiation between those multiple power centers. Where that does not occur, we have
problems." The process is tedious and often frustrating,
but it has paid off in community unity.

An example of a careful balancing of the city's multiple centers was the landslide passage of the drainage
bonds in 1983. The following year Cisneros served as the
mediating force in the balancing of interests that cleared
the way for a strategic new expressway at the western
edge of the city. While opening a vast area for upper income residential development in the northwest section of
the city, it also was designed to create opportunities for
new industry and jobs in the Edgewood Independent
School District in the heart of the poverty area on the
city's West Side. This required a series of meetings with
representatives of developers, school officials, and leaders
of Communities Organized for Public Service who spoke

for the Edgewood community.

Discussing his participation in such a process, Cisneros observes: "It's a different conception of the role of the mayor from in the past when you basically sold the business community [on a project] and then did it." Now, he explains, there is "an environment where the mayor is sort of the arbitrator . . . a mediating person between different centers of power—always with a personal agenda in mind, of course, but leaving that, in some sense, secondary to the process."

This vision of an expanded modern role for his office is tailor-made for a mayor with the irrepressible energy and long-range vision of Cisneros. His zest for action could not have been contained within the traditional job description. Instead, the mayor's absorption in economic development, community dialogue, and policy planning has left City Manager Lou Fox ample breathing space to perform his charter duties as chief administrator.

Fox, who had been assistant manager, was the mayor's personal choice to succeed Tom Huebner who had been losing council support and resigned suddenly in the fall of 1981. Fox had overwhelming council support and Cisneros moved to have him immediately voted manager-designate without any search.

"We've hit a very good accommodation," reported Cisneros after three years of working with Fox. "To put it in the simplest terms, it's 'Mr. Inside' and 'Mr. Outside.' Essentially it is my job to worry about the whole external environment in which we operate—politics, the council, community disputes, the national economy, companies coming in, the projection of the city's image, all that. And Lou, then, is in charge of the daily operations of the city and the system works well. No one crowds his turf."

This productive arrangement, however, is not possible without support from the City Council. San Antonio's city charter gives the mayor no real power. About the only power he has beyond that given other council members is the authority to call special meetings on his own initiative. A mayor must generate authority through his own political skills and Cisneros has met the challenge without noticeable strain—despite the rambunctious style of several council members whose performances have made cable broadcasts of meetings a popular form of soap opera.

At times some council members seem to consciously try to caricature themselves. For a while there was one member who delighted in dressing for public occasions in an Uncle Sam suit. More recently a member has made points with his constituents by occasionally donning a lion suit.

In dealing with the council, Cisneros is well aware of important assets that go with his position, even if they are not written into law. "One very important tool," he explains, "is the power to set the agenda—not only setting the mood within the council, but in the community . . . I can talk to the press on a given day and suddenly a new item has been interjected on the city agenda. That's a very important tool that can never be described in any charter." For the most part, however, the mayor's approach is more subtle and gradual than sudden. He periodically provides the council with the agenda he hopes to achieve over the next few months and he tries to stay in contact with members as it is developed.

The close contact he maintains with influential members, in fact, is an important element in what Cisneros sees as the second major tool which must be wielded by a successful mayor. This is the ability to put majorities together. After nearly four years of presiding over council meetings, Cisneros is able to count on a solid bloc of votes for his position on most issues of significance.

His key ally, perhaps, is Councilman Frank Wing, a Hispanic with Chinese antecedents who has emerged in recent years as one of the strongest and most stable leaders on the South Side of the city. Wing, who grew up in a

gang-ridden public housing project, followed the route of
many upward-bound Hispanics by enlisting in the Air
Force while he was a freshman in high school. He finished
high school while in service and later earned a college
degree while holding down a responsible U.S. Civil Service
post. He now is a top-ranking productivity specialist with
the Logistics Research and Systems Division of Kelly Air
Force Base. He has sided with Cisneros on several controversial growth and development issues, despite pressure
from Communities Organized for Public Service which
has strong influence in his district.

Cisneros combines his ability to fashion council
majorities for his major initiatives with a sure sense of
timing. As a result, he rarely has lost a council vote after
he has staked out a position.

This success at coalition-building has come as a surprise to some observers. Cisneros is frank to admit that he
had to deal with some "very skeptical" council members
when he first became mayor. "Their attitude essentially
was," he has recalled, "that 'we'll go along with the office
of mayor, but we're going to have to be persuaded about
the person [who holds it].' So I had some proving to do and
I was exceedingly careful for the first year or so."

One of the mysteries of public life is the way good luck
seems to attend the activities of some fortunate politicians. This has been the case with Cisneros in his years as
mayor. His job has been made easier because he has had
no serious challenger for leadership on the council.

There had been considerable speculation that with
the departure of Mayor Cockrell, Councilman Eureste, a
college social work professor with strong ties to COPS and
a network of alliances with minority council members,
might become a dominant behind-the-scenes force.
Eureste, a colorful and impetuous politician, had emerged
as leader of Texas delegates backing Senator Edward
Kennedy at the 1980 Democratic National Convention.

The question of whether he might mount a serious   89

challenge to Cisneros became moot, however, in February 1983, when Eureste and a woman graduate student were mugged while sitting in a parked car late one night in San Antonio's sprawling Brackenridge Park. One of the noisy dramas that enliven San Antonio politics at regular intervals then unfolded at City Hall over a period of weeks— almost crowding the National Municipal League's selection of San Antonio as an All-America City off the TV screens and front pages.

Eureste had been feuding with the Police Department before the incident and from a hospital where he received treatment following the mugging, he suggested that police officers had somehow been behind the attack, and went on to suggest he had been victim of an assassination attempt.

An outraged Cisneros denounced Eureste and withdrew support for his reelection, accusing him of trying to dodge responsibility for his actions in the affair. Eureste snapped back that the mayor was "two-faced," but a few days later he sheepishly issued an apology to the community and to the Police Department. But that wasn't the end of skirmishes between Eureste and Cisneros. A month later it was disclosed by the press that the irrepressible councilman had written a lengthy memorandum to the mayor in which he did not stint critical comments. Eureste has continued to launch challenges to Cisneros at intervals. Cisneros, in turn, hasn't hesitated to return fire.

In part, this is probably due to their differing political styles. While the mayor follows a consensus-building strategy, Eureste doesn't shrink from confrontation. But despite occasional hot rhetoric, the two have generally maintained friendly, if wary, relations.

In the 1983 election, while Cisneros was piling up his 94.2 percent of the vote, Eureste was forced into a runoff in his district. His opponent proved to be a political novice, and the controversial incumbent slipped back into office. His potential as challenger to the mayor, however, had been reduced drastically.

Despite hot words, Cisneros is well aware of Eureste's intellectual force and has been careful to work with him as much as possible. He even included him in a blanket endorsement of all 10 members of the council for re-election as the 1985 campaign season approached.

The Cisneros landslide in the city election of April 1983 was the inevitable outcome of a carefully-mounted campaign. The mayor's opposition was weak and frag-mented and he could easily have won with a minimal effort. But Cisneros was well aware that his ability to move his agenda through the City Council rises and falls with the level of his own popularity with voters. On the rare occasions when his community support had suffered a momentary slip, he could sense a lowering of his authority with the council. As the election approached, he was developing a long-range program of goals for the city and he knew that a successful campaign would provide the momentum he needed to launch it.

So, while he could scarcely have been described as "running scared," his reelection campaign was consid-erably more than a minimal effort. And, as he had planned, the massive victory solidified his authority at City Hall and confirmed his emerging status as the most effective political leader in South Texas.

It also cleared the way for a full-scale move into Dem-ocratic Party politics. A tradition of the Good Government League councils, though it was not always fully honored, was to shun involvement in county and state politics. In his years as a councilman Cisneros had given support to a few primary candidates, including U.S. Representative Albert Bustamante when he was making a successful challenge of the establishment in a race for County Judge. But he had stayed clear of most partisan politics.

91

The non-partisan approach played well in his first campaign for mayor. He undercut Steen's established strength in heavily Republican silk-stocking precincts when he spoke to a gathering of Republican women and pledged he would stay out of Democratic-Republican battles.

But this pledge kept Cisneros on the sidelines in the fall of 1982 when Texas Democrats went all out to defeat incumbent Governor Bill Clements, a close ally of President Ronald Reagan and the first Republican to hold the office in a century. When Governor Mark White upset Clements to complete a Democratic sweep of state offices, Cisneros could do no more than send congratulatory telegrams—a fact that was duly noted in party circles.

Accordingly, *Washington Post* correspondent Dan Balz struck a sensitive nerve when he wrote of grumbling by Democratic partisans that the mayor should "pay his dues." Cisneros soon advised friends that his non-partisanship pledge was not being renewed in his reelection campaign and he made the change formal when he announced in January 1983.

Almost immediately the mayor emerged as a leading figure in the Texas campaign for Walter Mondale. During a successful fund-raising visit to San Antonio on January 25 and 26, Mondale heaped praise on Cisneros, calling him "one of the truly exciting young political leaders in the United States today." The mayor's rising national profile was recognized on January 26 when he was chosen to respond to Reagan's State of the Union message on NBC's *Today Show* while Mondale was answering the president on *Good Morning America* from San Antonio's ABC outlet.

By the 1984 primary campaigns, Cisneros was ready to endorse around half a dozen state and area candidates. After the votes were counted on May 6, he could take satisfaction that all of them carried San Antonio and South Texas. He had established himself as a major player in Texas Democratic politics.⌉

By late April 1984, as the Texas caucuses emerged as a crucial test in the stormy campaign for the Democratic presidential nomination, Mondale was questioned during a San Antonio fund-raising visit about the possibility that Cisneros might become his running mate. "I'm not picking a vice president yet," responded Mondale, "but Henry Cisneros is certainly one of the most gifted young leaders in America today. My admiration for him is well known."

Mondale's admiration grew even greater a few days later when he rode the primary election polls with the mayor and swept the San Antonio caucuses that night. While most Texas observers were following an early script that made Senator Lloyd Bentsen (architect of the party's 1982 statewide sweep), the logical choice for the vice presidential nomination, Cisneros was making a deep impression on the front-running candidate and his staff. A few weeks later came the invitation to North Oaks, Minnesota.

Cisneros was aware that his emergence as an active player at the level of national politics would have a downside. He knew that there would be a reaction from conservative voters; at the same time he was well aware that his certification as a national leader would strengthen his image at home. And he was careful not to let national activities distract him from the business at hand at City Hall.

VIII

Super-Mayor

The high approval ratings which placed Cisneros in a strong position to expand his national political role were built on a record of skillful solutions to problems which could have split the city.

The most difficult was a long-festering controversy over San Antonio's deep involvement in the South Texas Nuclear Project (STP). When Cisneros assumed office, the project was far behind schedule, far above cost estimates, and a prime target of anti-nuclear activists. City Public Service had joined in the project in 1973 with Houston Lighting and Power Company (HL&P), Central Power and Light Company, based in Corpus Christi, and the City of Austin. CPS assumed a 28 percent share.

Construction by Brown & Root, Inc., which also was assigned design responsibility as architect/engineer, began in late 1975 with a cost estimate of $1.1 billion. By August 1979, the estimated cost had risen to $2.7 billion. Controversy mounted in 1980 when the Nuclear Regulatory Commission found procedural problems and inadequacies in the work. By the time Mayor Cisneros took office, an independent study for the STP partners had produced a gloomy report, citing serious shortcomings in the work.

Almost immediately, the new mayor was under heavy pressure from COPS which argued that because of rising electric rates to pay for STP, many low-income San Antonians were having to choose between food and utility service. The powerful neighborhood organization called upon the City Council to take steps to limit the city's participation in the project.

The mayor, who had established himself as a consistent supporter of the nuclear plant, followed a characteristic strategy. Through a broad-based advisory committee, he set the wheels in motion for a long-range "San Antonio Energy Study" by outside technical consultants; they were asked to review the existing energy strategy of CPS and go on to define a long-range energy program for the city. At the same time Cisneros demonstrated a willingness to consider proposals for reducing or selling San Antonio's share, but he demanded answers to tough questions regarding alternative sources of energy and comparative costs. Meanwhile, he continued to hold a Council majority behind participation in the project— even after Austin voters adopted a proposal calling for sale of their city's share in STP, a move which attracted no interested buyers.

Another familiar Cisneros strategy was the staging of public hearings on energy matters, allowing hours of complaints and arguments from the public. Cisneros was playing a double role in the long controversy, since as mayor he serves as an ex officio member of the City Public Service Board. While the board has independent decision-making authority, the council has an effective veto through its crucial role in approving necessary bond sales and rate increases.

The STP crisis lasted through the mayor's first year in office. During that time, Cisneros emerged as a leader, as the minority partners forced changes through HL&P, the managing partner. Brown & Root was replaced as architect/engineer by the Bechtel Energy Corporation, and then B&R resigned also as contractor in late 1981. Construction stopped and was not resumed until June 1982, several months after Ebasco Constructors, Inc. was appointed new contractor.

In August 1982, Bechtel issued a new cost forecast of $5.495 billion which has proved to be firm. Work shifted to a greatly accelerated schedule in 1984. In May 1983, the San Antonio Energy Study was completed by Boston area consultants and concluded that the South Texas Project should result in lower costs to the electric system and to consumers over the long term. The study also recommended a number of conservation measures and energy options favored by Cisneros. These are being put into place.

In a city whose voters had made rising energy costs an explosive political issue for over a decade, Cisneros— with the help of a slim council majority—had managed to remove electric rates and nuclear controversy from the active political agenda.

If the long battle over the nuclear plant demonstrated that Cisneros could resist the populist pressures of COPS and other critics of City Public Service, another controversy showed that he would not hesitate to take on the city's business establishment. At stake was the critical question of who would provide the city's supply of natural gas—a hypersensitive issue in view of the political trauma that accompanied the swift escalation of gas prices in the 1970's and San Antonio's bitter fight with its supplier at the time.

The settlement of the legal war with Coastal States brought about the creation of Valero Energy Corporation with headquarters in San Antonio to replace LoVaca, the Coastal subsidiary which had serviced South Texas. When Cisneros became mayor, the gas supply contract inherited by Valero was about to expire. Cisneros called this situation "unacceptable," arguing that unless a new contract were achieved, consumers would be at the mercy of prices determined solely by Valero and the Texas Railroad Commission. Again his strategy was to go to a citizens committee, including gas exploration and energy experts, to study alternative sources. In early 1982 the committee, headed by Trinity University President Ronald Calgaard, recommended that City Public Service begin an aggressive campaign to locate a natural gas supplier to offer competition to Valero.

For a time the prospects for real competition for the San Antonio market appeared dim. There was no response to efforts by CPS staffers to attract bids.

Then the economic recession took a hand, causing a steady decline in demand for natural gas, especially from petrochemical plants in the Gulf Coast area. In midsummer of 1982, officials of the huge Houston Pipe Line Company, seeking to beef up lagging sales, took note of the San Antonio situation and contacted CPS. By December, Houston Pipe Line was proposing to supply one half of San Antonio's needs which were running at the rate of $245 million a year. At its meeting that month, the City Public Service Board voted to split the contract. Houston Pipe Line President Jim Walzel was aware of the City Council's veto power over CPS matters, so he wisely sought the added approval of the council, setting the stage for a classic political struggle between the mayor and Valero, a hometown corporation.

Cisneros won a qualified victory in the first skirmish. In early January he was able to win a council vote directing the city staff and CPS trustees to seek a contract with Houston Pipe Line as the city's second supplier. But the decision came only after a stormy seven-hour debate in which it became clear that the mayor had a slim one-vote majority for the change. In addition, the council delayed

97

final action for forty-five days and called for a study by expert consultants.

Even before the first council showdown, the battle for public opinion had been joined. A delegation of Valero employees delivered a petition signed by 800 of the corporation's San Antonio staff to the mayor, challenging the economic assumptions of the plan and asserting that it "seems our politicians are intent upon a decision that can only harm the growth and development of San Antonio." Cisneros responded he was concerned with the welfare of the Valero employees but also was concerned about the 2,000 CPS customers whose utilities were disconnected monthly because they could not afford to pay their bills.

The debate raged for weeks with most leaders of the business community siding with Valero and stressing its credentials as an asset to the city. For a time the battle shifted to the Texas Legislature where Valero's friends on the San Antonio delegation promoted legislation which would have had the effect of forcing Houston Pipe Line out of the competition. Cisneros and his allies, including Mrs. Cockrell (who had been appointed to the CPS board after leaving the mayor's office), won a major victory when the study by National Economic Research Associates of Washington, D.C., recommended that the contract be split.

It was not enough. In mid-April the council voted 6-5 to give a twenty-year contract to Valero which had sweetened its proposal by agreeing to deliver spot market gas purchased by CPS in amounts ranging up to 20 percent of the city's requirements. Again the debate was long and stormy, but the mayor's impassioned arguments could not hold his slim margin from the previous vote. Calling the vote a step backward, he told the council that Valero "came in asking for supper and you are giving them the whole dinner table."

Even so, Cisneros, with help from Mrs. Cockrell and other trustees of CPS, was able to press for better terms than charted by the council, raising several alternatives that might be pursued by the board. As a result, the final agreement reached by CPS with its gas supplier provided for a five-year contract. Valero agreed to transport gas from alternative lower-priced sources, in amounts ranging up to about 25 percent of San Antonio's average daily needs.

Reviewing the fight many months later, Cisneros had become somewhat philosophic about the outcome. He discussed the "full court press" mounted by the business community and explained that "they couldn't understand why I was doing what I was doing. . . . They just couldn't explain my behavior."

The problem was in communications. Many members of the business elite, Cisneros observed, "don't understand it when I say the reason I am pro-business and pro-economic development is because I want to help people who have been outside of the mainstream. They think that is just words. All they concentrate on is the fact that I am generally pro-business and they assume I am just pro-business for the sake of it like everyone else."

His approach to the gas contract was not anti-business as some critics suggested. "The point of the matter was," Cisneros said, "that the same agenda that drives my pro-business stance was driving this: a better deal for people who are poor."

Some business leaders finally understood the mayor's position but did not agree with him. "They fought me on it and they beat me," he said, reviewing the battle which resulted in the switching of sides by one of the mayor's original backers on the council.

Actually the mayor might well have claimed a qualified victory. In its annual report for the year ending January 31, 1984 (covering about eight months of the new agreement), CPS reported its purchases from "alternate suppliers" were running about $1 per thousand cubic feet   99 lower than Valero's price. It estimated that savings to consumers over the first five years would be in excess of $70 million.

"Perhaps it worked out for the best," commented Cisneros. "We got our break in price and Valero remained the major supplier—the hometown company . . . so I'm not bitter about it."

Inevitably, the extraordinary growth in the role of the mayor during the two Cisneros terms and his emphasis on including a broad spectrum of the community in the decision-making process has imposed great strain on a City Hall apparatus which had not been designed to meet such demands. The mayor inherited a remarkably able administrative assistant, Shirl Thomas, from Mrs. Cockrell. She manages to monitor progress of a host of the mayor's initiatives, while supervising his tiny staff and attending to arrangements for conventions and the growing retinue of visiting dignitaries. But a staff of four simply isn't enough to handle the whole load.

The heaviest pressure has centered on the mayor's schedule. Demands on his time have been extraordinary ever since the night he was first elected, and they have multiplied since his work on the Kissinger Commission, his appearance on *Sixty Minutes*, and his consideration for the Democratic vice presidential nomination. Despite his 12- to 16-hour days, there is not time for all of the speeches, interviews, and meetings proposed for him. But the mayor has been slow to restrict his appointments to a realistic level. The resulting overscheduling has led to cancellations and traffic jams that have sometimes been damaging—at least politically.

In his second term as mayor, Cisneros has made an effort to get control of his schedule and to make time for himself and his family. Barbie Hernandez, who keeps his calendar, tries to set aside three two-hour segments each week for Cisneros to jog. Normally, he runs three or four miles around the track at Lanier High School in his neighborhood. Often his wife and daughters go with him. Sometimes late in the evening he will run cross-country through the West Side and stop by his parents' home and visit with them over a bowl of ice cream.

In order to keep up his brutal pace, Cisneros regularly exercises and watches what he eats. He gave up coffee years ago because the caffeine made him edgy and irritable; now he drinks tea instead. Careful about cholesterol, he eats one egg a week, no more, no less. As a rule, he doesn't drink hard liquor, and only occasionally drinks wine or beer with dinner.

Mary Alice tries not to allow Henry's frantic schedule to disrupt the whole family. Basically, they live a normal middle-class existence. Instead of eating out at fancy restaurants, Henry and Mary Alice take the girls to McDonald's or to pizza parlors. They don't take expensive out-of-state vacations, choosing instead to get away for a few days at a time on the Gulf Coast of Texas. They regularly go to Mass as a family at Sacred Heart Catholic Church, located in the heart of the West Side. Both daughters attend Catholic schools. On Thanksgiving and Christmas, they visit both Henry's parents and Mary Alice's.

A day with the mayor makes it easy to understand his scheduling problem. We chose a quiet midsummer day to follow him. Cisneros arrived at his office at 8:30 A.M., garbed in what has become his uniform—a dark suit, blue button-down shirt and conservative maroon tie. He was lugging a hefty briefcase filled with his overnight homework.

He went into an immediate session with his four staffers. They ran through his schedule for the day and then began to deal with correspondence, his ongoing monthly agenda, and long lists of matters requiring decisions. The group sat comfortably around a coffee table in his office, but Cisneros was all business. His attention to detail never wavered as he probed the staff with quiet questions.

The mayor gave brief instructions: "Send a little note on this to Senator [Richard] Lugar. . . . I've known him since National League of Cities days." He picked up a memorial booklet and instructed, "This deserves a nice note." Then he opened a file and advised, "I've got a bunch of economic development letters here, but they need my personal attention. I wasn't able to get to them on the plane."

They moved into a discussion of a controversy over apparent shortcomings in the 911 emergency telephone system. (Funds to upgrade the system were included in the new city budget a few months later.) Then Cisneros discussed plans for an economic development trip to Dallas and a day in Austin with state and municipal officials, including Governor Mark White.

A call from Councilman Ed Harrington, a key member of the mayor's team, interrupted the session and Cisneros briefed him on a memo he was sending the council on the monthly agenda. Hanging up, Cisneros observed, "O.K., we've got a little time. Ed's not coming in."

Then it was back to lists and memorandums. At intervals, the mayor would advise, "I guess that's it," and move on to other business. He glanced at a request that he testify before a Congressional committee. "That's one more out-of-town commitment I don't need," he said, turning it down.

It wasn't until nearly 10 A.M. that the mayor was able to announce. "O.K., folks, that's the lot." He moved to his big, uncluttered desk and signed correspondence and answered a reporter's questions until it was time for a one-hour radio call-in show. Talking from his desk he fielded a barrage of questions flawlessly, moving easily from topic to topic. At the close of the session, he was available to enlarge on some of his answers for City Hall reporters who had been monitoring the show. He talked to another councilman by phone and then held an impromptu press conference over the 911 problem and a temporary snag in the plan for a new Northwest Expressway.

Then it was time to leave for the luncheon of the San Antonio Manufacturers Association at the Lone Star Brewery where he was scheduled as speaker. While his Police Department driver negotiated traffic, the mayor pored over the morning mail. At the meeting he moved easily through the buffet line, greeting members by name. At 12:40 P.M. he rose to speak and reviewed a long list of important matters on the City Hall agenda with emphasis on the city's need for a surface water supply to meet long-range needs and on the importance of the forthcoming special session of the Texas Legislature on education.

Back at City Hall he went immediately into a conference with the city manager and then upstairs to a session of a community-wide committee on literacy problems. When it ended, it was mid-afternoon and the mayor went directly to his office. First there was a meeting with representatives of the San Antonio Festival, an annual international music event that began in 1983. Next, he saw a group working on seed capital for a business training center in an urban development project.

By then it was 5 P.M. and City Hall was emptying, but Cisneros stayed at his desk, making phone calls and clearing up the day's loose ends. At 6 P.M. he headed home with his briefcase again filled with homework. For Cisneros it had been a light day. More often than not he goes on to an evening engagement that may last two to three hours.

The final test for a mayor, of course, is public acceptance. In the fall of 1983, a poll of 510 voting households in Bexar County, including San Antonio, probed opinions about government. The results were striking. The city's leadership, represented by the mayor and City Council, received what were described as "phenomenally high marks." Eighty percent of those questioned judged the council's job performance as either good or excellent. The mark of excellent was given by 36.6 percent.

This represented a remarkable reversal of findings in polls taken for John Steen in 1977, 1979, and 1981—just prior to his race for mayor. In none did the City Council receive favorable ratings from more than one-third of those questioned.

Political observers are convinced that the change in perception was tied directly to the leadership of Cisneros. With one exception, the same council members were in office. The mayor's skillful projection of the city's image as a unified community on the move to greatness had changed the public view of city government.

Trinity University political science professor Tucker Gibson, who did polling and consulting for Steen, has been impressed by the ability of Cisneros to develop effective coalitions. "I'm struck by the continuity of the coalitions that have supported Cisneros," he says. "But it is personalized. It is centered on him." No broad political organization comparable to the old Good Government League has formed around the mayor. "He's got his antennae up and he's very sensitive," says Gibson. "His leadership style is highly individualistic, rather than institutional."

Meanwhile, the mayor's swift rise to national prominence has quite naturally led to speculation on who will be able to follow his virtuoso performance. It is a subject of special concern to the business community.

Whenever he does make his expected move for state or federal office, the problem of attracting suitable competitors to fill the vacancy at City Hall is likely to lead to a charter amendment providing a serious salary for future mayors.

IX

The Central
American Caper

For about a week after President Reagan named him as one of twelve members of his National Bipartisan Commission on Central America on July 19, 1983, Henry Cisneros had a problem sleeping.

"I kept having nightmares of people being marched into ovens and catacombs, and of blood-flowing rivers and beheadings," he told us. "I'd wake up in the middle of the night and I'd see people being chopped up with machetes and things like that! Frankly, I felt like it was beyond my control. I thought, 'How in the world could I have been so stupid as to get involved in this thing?' because I felt like a moth being drawn to the flame." The dreams seemed to tell him, "You are beyond your powers and you are going to be burned. . . ."

The dreams, no doubt, were an outgrowth of his heritage. "I'm a Hispanic," he said. "There are levels of the mystical in one's personality. . . . The Aztecs had a real mysticism about them and Mexican history is full of just horror. I mean, look at the murals of Orozco and you will find the ghosts from the conquest . . . you know, murder and mass slavery and beheadings and parts being pulled out of people while they're still alive. Just horrible." He was underlining historic and cultural realities that form a barrier to understanding of the region by Americans.

The commission, headed by former Secretary of State Henry A. Kissinger, was appointed at a time of increasing tension and controversy over the administration's policy for dealing with the guerrilla challenge in El Salvador and with the Marxist Sandinista government of Nicaragua which it accused of spreading revolution through Central America.

President Reagan announced the members of the Kissinger Commission after using an observance of Captive Nations Week to stress his view of developments in Central America as part of a larger struggle between East and West. "We see the Soviets and Cuba building a war machine in Nicaragua that dwarfs the forces of all their neighbors combined," he said. "It is being built, by their own boasts, to impose a revolution without frontiers."

Ominously, newspapers reporting the appointment of the commission also reported that the Pentagon had ordered an eight-ship aircraft carrier battle group to change course from a western Pacific destination and take up stations off the Pacific Coast of Central America. A few days later, newsmen were briefed on elaborate plans for maneuvers in Honduras involving Army and Marine troops with Navy tactical air support.

They were told a battle group centered on the carrier *Coral Sea* would move into the Caribbean. The maneuvers which were to continue into January were designed, it was reported, to deter Nicaragua from aggression and dissuade its government from fomenting insurrections.

Meanwhile, the administration was reported to be preparing an expansion of support for the Contra forces in Nicaragua—the anti-Sandinista insurgents supplied and supported by the Central Intelligence Agency.

All of this came at a time of growing doubts in Congress over administration policy, and increasing opposition to our covert support of the Contras.

There were doubts, too, about the role of the commission. Kissinger was seen as viewing the world in stark East-West terms, and Latin Americans recalled he was Secretary of State when the Chilean military overthrew the elected leftist government of Chile in 1973. Some administration officials privately conceded that, while the panel was a bipartisan and independent body, it had been chosen with an eye toward promoting the administration's policies.

Certainly the White House must have felt secure in the appointment of Cisneros, a moderate big-city mayor who had remained largely on the fringe of Democratic Party affairs, a representative of Hispanics who would be unlikely to make waves. If so, the White House was wrong.

On August 10, the day set for the swearing-in of the Kissinger Commission, a story from San Antonio by *Washington Post* writer David Hoffman was page one news. It detailed the deep reservations held by Cisneros about President Reagan's Central American policies.

Disagreeing with the administration analysis placing the Soviets and Cuba at the core of the problem, Cisneros warned:

"What we do need to fear is continuing a history by which we lose the people. And that history has taken the form of military intervention, it has taken the form of toppling governments that we don't favor, it's taken the form of economic exploitation by companies, it's taken the form of rigging elections and I think we have to fundamentally change our role."

Warning that "we are not perceived as peacemakers, but instead as heavy-handed," Cisneros observed, "The United States generally is in a poor position to be either the solution to the problem alone, or even to aspire to lead   107 negotiations because of our long history in the region." He called on the United States to respect self-determination in the region even if the result was distasteful, while at the same time he said the Soviets and Cubans must also respect self-determination.

Without consciously intending it, Cisneros had staked out the role he would play on the commission—one of close and determined questioning of the conventional wisdom presented by many of the witnesses before the commission. And almost immediately he felt the response from conservative members of the group.

"It was a strange experience in a way," observes Cisneros, "because the usual criticism against me is for being too much of a diplomat, too much of a crafter of language or a consensus-builder—too much of that. And here I could tell by body language and comment that I was perceived as the wild, flaming, uncontrollable bomb-throwing member of the group."

The sharp differences in position between Cisneros and outspoken conservatives on the committee were drawn publicly on the night of their first meeting when Cisneros appeared on the *MacNeil-Lehrer Report* with Dr. John Silber, president of Boston University, and Dr. William B. Walsh, president and director of Project Hope. Their disagreements were not destined to fade away.

At the end of August, the commission held meetings with such prominent figures as former Secretaries of State Cyrus Vance, Alexander M. Haig, Jr., and Dean Rusk, and former Presidents Gerald Ford and Jimmy Carter. Their testimony was predictable.

Vance said problems in Central America were more the result of local conditions than outside agitation by the Soviets and Cuba, and said a political solution was "clearly preferable" to military solutions. In direct contrast, Haig told reporters the problem "is first and foremost global, second regional with focus on Cuba, and third it is local." Carter said the United States should work very closely with other countries in the region in seeking to alleviate social and economic hardships and to prevent subversion. Later in September, former President Nixon called for a bold economic plan in Latin America that would cost more than the post-World War II Marshall Plan for Europe.

Cisneros prepared for his role on the commission in characteristically careful fashion. He regularly met with scholars from the University of Texas at San Antonio and Trinity University who had knowledge of the region. He was briefed by Archbishop Patrick Flores and Catholic priests with extensive ties in the area. Cisneros had been to Mexico many times and had made trips to Guatemala and Honduras, but realized he had much to learn about the Central American situation. On the other hand, he had devoted a considerable amount of study at Harvard to economic development in the Third World—one of the most important subjects on the commission's agenda.

He came away from the committee's hearings and deliberations more than ever convinced of the importance of economic development in the quest for peace. "If you want to make peace in the Third World," he said, "then help the people eat and take care of their children and [help them] have schools and clinics and roads and dams and rural electrification."

Given the philosophical tilt of the commission members, which ranged from moderate to conservative, Cisneros, a political moderate himself, felt an obligation to raise questions and points of view that otherwise might be neglected. "I felt," he says, "that I had to in some sense be provocative and make sure the left's point of view was at least tested."

Cisneros found himself allied to Carlos F. Diaz-Alejandro, a Yale professor, whose appointment to the commission had been protested by conservatives. Inevitably there was friction.

Silber, a strong-willed philosopher-administrator who himself had grown up in San Antonio, needled the two Hispanics by referring to them as Commandante Cisneros and Commandante Diaz, a reminder of the titles carried by Sandinista leaders. Walsh would shake his head and make faces when Cisneros was speaking. "All I was trying to do," the mayor says, "was force another view . . . when we had witnesses before us who were showing no balance at all."

In the end, Cisneros says, testimony from Amnesty International was so authentic and graphic that it forced the commission to come around—at least in the matter of death-squad terror. "When Amnesty International came and gave us the names and the parents and the book of all the disappearances in Salvador in a month . . . and it was 440 in a month . . . and they had the manner of death, how they were found. . . . It was like 'the victim was found in a road with a machete slash and his head off because he was a union organizer' . . . there came a point where they just couldn't deny the existence of death squads."

Despite his skeptical attitude in commission deliberations, Cisneros developed a productive relationship with Kissinger, even though he suspects the former Secretary of State was wary initially. "He had no idea about my makeup," says Cisneros, adding Kissinger probably "thought they had saddled him with a real wild card." In any event, Cisneros feels he received more than routine attention from the chairman who seemed to make a point of including him in key private meetings, such as one he held with President Miguel de la Madrid Hurtado of Mexico. Cisneros was aware, of course, that the master negotiator's attention may have been designed to neutralize him.

At the same time he was awed by Kissinger's sheer intellectual power. "He has a phenomenal recall for detail," reports Cisneros, "a tremendous capacity to take

110   a fact situation which has three or four elements and

paint a generalizable picture, which is not only a practical picture but is buttressed by theory, and compare it to a situation that happened, say, in 1643."

During the commission's whirlwind trip through six countries of Central America in six days, Kissinger displayed immense energy. "He would flat run us into the ground," Cisneros said. "He would get up before anybody else. We would go through our regular schedule all day and would quit about 10 P.M. and I would notice his schedule called for a final meeting with the head of that government at dinner at 10."

Cisneros was similarly impressed by two leading Democrats on the commission, AFL-CIO President Lane Kirkland and Robert Strauss, the Texan who had served as chairman of the Democratic National Committee for five years and was President Carter's personal representative in Middle East negotiations from 1979-81.

"Kissinger was afraid of one man," reports Cisneros, "and that was Lane Kirkland. If Kirkland had bolted, the commission would have been a failure."

Praising Kirkland's intellectual grasp and his diplomatic presence, Cisneros observes, "He knows virtually every head of state in the world," adding that he is at the same level as Kissinger in this regard. More important, perhaps, is Kirkland's centrist philosophy as a graduate of the "George Meany school of foreign policy."

"We just say thank God that the American labor movement is the centrist movement it is and not a polarized movement like Great Britain's," says Cisneros, arguing that U.S. labor has provided "one of the stable anchors of our foreign policy."

The commission's trip to Central America began with a day in Panama on October 10, followed by visits of one day each in Costa Rica, El Salvador, Guatemala, Honduras, and Nicaragua.

Almost immediately Cisneros found himself protest- 111

ing an incident in which three members of the commission met with Alfonso Robledo Callejas, a key leader of the Revolutionary Democratic Alliance, one of the Contra guerrilla groups engaged in action against the Sandinista government of Nicaragua. It had been understood the commission would not meet with rebel groups and the commission had declined to meet with Guillermo Manuel Ungo, a top leader of the Salvadoran Revolutionary Democratic Front.

When the meeting with Robledo was confirmed to him by a correspondent of the *Los Angeles Times*, Cisneros reminded Kissinger "that it was a violation of our understanding." Kissinger agreed. There were no more meetings with rebels during the trip and Ungo, a former vice presidential running mate of Salvadoran President Jose Napoleon Duarte, later was granted a session in Washington.

One of the most dramatic moments of the commission's meetings came during its brief visit to El Salvador when members met with Roberto d'Aubuisson, leader of the right-wing coalition, who had been accused of having links with death squads. Death-squad violence was a matter of urgent concern to Kirkland because of the murder of two AFL-CIO field workers in El Salvador and of the failure of the government to bring their killers to justice.

Kirkland did not hesitate to confront d'Aubuisson in blunt and direct fashion. As he did so, Cisneros recalls, "the lights went out, so the room darkened at that instant." There was a sense that "evil was descending." It was, Cisneros says, "quite a moment."

D'Aubuisson denied involvement with the death squads, blaming the army. As the session was ending, he approached Cisneros and spoke to him in Spanish, proposing, "Let's go have a drink, I want to talk to you." Cisneros prudently evaded, saying "I'll get back to you later." Chuckling as he described the conversation, Cisneros said, "I didn't like the idea of riding around in a car

with him."

Cisneros could not escape reminders of death squads in El Salvador. People came to him at his hotel to tell him about the violence. The rector of a university told of students who had disappeared or been frightened into going into hiding. He was told about the newspaper advertisements used by the right wing to target their opponents for death-squad attention.

"They wouldn't talk in the room," said Cisneros. "We'd go for a walk . . . pretty weird."

The commission's visit to Nicaragua was not a public relations success for the Sandinistas. The negatives started at the airport where there was no official reception and the press and others were allowed to swarm around Kissinger. "The Secret Service had to push people just so he could walk," said Cisneros. "There was no protection. It was like, 'Welcome to Nicaragua, you son of a bitch.' It was dangerous because we were all getting pushed around. . . . It was stupid on the part of the Nicaraguans, childish."

The visit was typified by the commission's session with Daniel Ortega Saavedra, the head of state, who harangued them in browbeating fashion for forty-five minutes. Kissinger stood up, Cisneros recalled, and said, "I resent the tone of your remarks, your personal attack on me, and your indecency toward my country. Thank you very much."

"And that," said Cisneros, laughing, "was the end of it."

In December, commission members met with Mexican President Miguel de la Madrid Hurtado and Foreign Minister Bernardo Sepulveda Amor. De la Madrid had been pressing the efforts of the Contadora group—Mexico, Venezuela, Colombia, and Panama—to bring about a negotiated solution to Central America's problems. "I learned a lot from de la Madrid," reports Cisneros, who was included in a private meeting with the Mexican president in which the Contadora process was discussed.

That same month the commission got down to working on its report. Almost immediately there were reports   113 of a sharp split over the question of making U.S. aid to El Salvador conditional on halting the violence of right-wing death squads. Strauss and Kirkland were insisting on conditionality of aid, against Kissinger's opposition.

Even so, the sessions had light moments which relaxed tension. Strauss and Kissinger in particular indulged in humorous by-play. "Strauss would come out with all kinds of stuff," Cisneros recalls, laughing about his Texas stories and expressions. "These guys are hilarious. They would keep the group in stitches and then they'd take off on each other and it would go on for fifteen minutes, a digression into stories about people they knew."

Preceded by extensive leaks, the commission's report was presented on Wednesday, January 11. The showdown had been on the previous Thursday when Kissinger reluctantly agreed to Kirkland's insistence on human rights conditions on aid. But late the following afternoon Kissinger delivered a strenuous objection from the White House which argued the provision would interfere with progress already being made. Kirkland held firm. Without the human rights condition, he wouldn't sign the report. He won the battle of wills.

Kissinger, joined by Silber and former Senator Nicholas F. Brady, signed a dissenting footnote calling upon Congress and the executive branch to avoid interpreting "conditionality in a manner that leads to a Marxist-Leninist victory in El Salvador. . . ."

In the end, Cisneros signed the report, but added his own dissenting footnotes. He was strongly influenced in his decision to sign by counselling from Strauss. "I had to really wrestle with tough calls for me," the mayor reports. "Should I have declined to sign the report," he asks, "after having internally gotten a whole bunch of concessions— you know, softened language and moves into the middle— and then just said one day, 'I am hereby declining to sign

114

the report; I'm going to publish my own report'?"

Strauss provided a reminder, says Cisneros, that "effectiveness in this setting involves not only what you say, but whether you are perceived to have been fair and procedurally correct." The point was to get your message across, but not be dismissed and have the message dismissed with you by people who would say, "Well, he had his mind made up from the outset." At the same time, Cisneros says he did not want to go as far as some liberals urged—people who would have said, "no aid to Salvador."

Cisneros, in fact, feels strongly about the importance of aid to Salvador. At the time of the report he felt that Jose Napoleon Duarte, whom he greatly admires as a true democrat, had a good chance to win the forthcoming election and would deserve and need U.S. assistance.

In a long footnote regarding El Salvador he called for "strong steps" to be taken to convince moderates within the rebel groups who had "backgrounds of peaceful political struggle" to take part in "discussions concerning participation in a security task force to arrange security provisions for all participants in election processes." He proposed that as a part of security arrangements the "Salvadoran security forces and the guerrillas should agree to a complete cease-fire and cessation of hostilities."

Cisneros was placing heavy emphasis on a process of dialogue. The discussions on details of security arrangements and elections, he wrote, "are intended to determine the extent to which meaningful dialogue on coalition approaches and structural reforms can proceed."

He also proposed a program of dialogue with the Sandinista regime in Nicaragua, urging that it be encouraged to work for "internal conciliation" with the Catholic Church, the private sector, and opposition parties. "I believe further accommodation by the Nicaraguan regime to its internal opposition and to its neighbors," Cisneros wrote, "can be encouraged through vigorous diplomacy by the United States."

In connection with this he urged that the United States "suspend 'covert' aid to the anti-Sandinista rebels" for a year "so that the Sandinista government can demonstrate its capacity to move toward pluralism and to fulfill its promise to hold free and fair elections in 1985." The suspension, he wrote, "is intended to be matched by significant movement on the part of the Nicaraguan government to change policies which have aroused apprehension among its regional neighbors and is intended to reduce the risk of war between Nicaragua and Honduras."

Discussing his position in late 1984, Cisneros felt he had emerged from his experience with the commission with much the same position as he started. "I don't think my position changed much," he said, recalling his early emphasis on standing for democracy and for economic development, arguing that "dialogue and negotiations are always better than armed conflict" and that support of the Contras was a mistake.

The Contra operation, he had concluded, had become a fundamental flaw in the administration's policy. Such operations "take on a life of their own" and cannot be easily switched off—even if U.S. diplomats achieve an understanding with the Sandinistas.

Cisneros was also satisfied that his position was well within the mainstream of the Democratic Party. He pointed out that at his meeting with Walter Mondale in North Oaks, Minnesota, they had discussed Central America, and Mondale was in complete agreement with him.

He talked to us at the time Duarte had opened a dialogue with rebel leaders in a mid-October meeting at La Palma. "I feel vindicated by the Duarte step," Cisneros said. "Vindicated because he's the right person doing the right thing."

Cisneros has remained in contact with Duarte whose son, the mayor of San Salvador, visited him in San Antonio in the fall of 1984 to appeal for support within the Democratic Party for aid to his country, and received a sympathetic response. Pointing out Duarte's long commitment to democracy, Cisneros asked us when it had "become a sin to get duly elected democratically and be allowed to survive."

The intensive exposure to the Central American problem has led Cisneros to draw some conclusions about the U.S. approach to the Third World. He is convinced that "the scale of what we do is wrong." Programs do not fit the stage of development of targeted nations. Cisneros explains:

"We send down massive bureaucratic structures, long pipelines, red tape—impersonal. I think if we're going to make a difference in that part of the world, it's going to revolve around, not the U.S. government and bureaucracy, but utilizing churches and private clinics and small efforts like the Peace Corps. And frankly one of the things we've not mastered as a country is what outreach we are going to have toward those countries. AID is not the answer, the traditional State Department method is not the answer, the United States Army is not the answer, the Corps of Engineers is not the answer."

Another problem in dealing with Latin America, he observes, is that "we insist on wanting to know the answers before we start the process," while "the Latin mentality is that what's important is the process—show respect in the process, give me time in the dialogue, let's work our way through it and down the road it will come out, but don't set the conditions in advance."

The United States must also, Cisneros believes, develop a "clear ideology that is relevant to the people of the region," and which counters the Marxist promise to "feed the people." He explains: "We have not found a way to effectively embody our democratic traditions in a way that is relevant to the Third World, particularly to the people of poor countries."

The answer, says Cisneros, is to be found in a serious dedication to democracy. "I am convinced," he says, "that 117

CISNEROS

if we have to stand for something, of all the choices that there are, we ought to stand simply for democracy. Fundamentally you start with democracy as a viable principle of government and you back people that stand for democracy. And that keeps us safe."

President Ronald Reagan meets with the Bipartisan Commission on Central America in the Cabinet Room in late October, 1983. Mayor Cisneros is toward the far end of the table, separated from the President by Robert Strauss and Henry Kissinger. (White House photo by Pete Souza)

Cartoonist John Branch took note of the strong reservations expressed by Cisneros over administration policies in Central America soon after he was named to the Bipartisan Commission.

A fund-raising reception in December 1983, at the home of supporter
Raul Jimenez, gave Cisneros an opportunity to praise Walter
Mondale on the eve of the 1984 primary battles. (*Express-News* photo
by Bob Owen)

A major initiative by Mayor Cisneros was the creation of a High Technology High School. He is shown congratulating the first graduates in a 1984 ceremony at City Hall. (*Express-News* photo by Jose Barrera)

The mayor receives members of the U.S. Pentathlon Team, shortly after they won a silver medal at the XXIII Olympics in Los Angeles. (Photo by Linda Palmer)

Henry Cisneros returned to Texas A & M University, from which he had graduated in 1968, to join Vice President George Bush and Governor Mark White in addressing the graduating class of 1984. (Texas A & M News Office)

Mayor Cisneros, in a restaurant apron, serves hamburgers to supporters during a fund-raising brunch in August 1984. (*Express-News* photo by Pat Sullivan)

The mayor meets his new colleagues in the Urban Studies Department of Trinity University: (from left) Catherine H. Powell, Dr. Heywood T. Sanders, and Dr. Earl M. Lewis, chairman. (Trinity University photo)

Mayor Cisneros joined residents of an East Side neighborhood in September, 1984, to hear their complaints about drug-dealing and prostitution. (*Express-News* photo by Joe Barrera, Jr.)

Breaking ground for a new business enterprise is one of the mayor's favorite occasions—especially when the development is in an area of high unemployment. (Photo by Catherine Cisneros)

The mayor's penchant for travel on the city's behalf is the subject of this Branch cartoon.

On July 4, 1984, Walter Mondale introduced Cisneros to his widest
audience yet. Mary Alice and the children accompanied the
mayor. Theresa (left) and Mercedes carried a gift basket of jalapeno
candy to North Oaks, Minnesota. (Wide World photo)

Henry Cisneros addressed a late-night session of the 1984 Democratic
National Convention in San Francisco. His theme was fairness.
(Photo by Catherine Cisneros)

Cisneros on the floor of the Democratic National Convention talks
with California Congressman Norman Mineta and his wife, May.
(UPI/Bettmann Archive)

The mayor accompanied Senator Ted Kennedy when he came to San Antonio on behalf of the Mondale-Ferraro ticket in October 1984. (*Express-News* photo by Scott Sines)

Mayor Cisneros pauses for reflection during a late October rally for the 1984 Democratic ticket. (*Express-News* photo by Pat Sullivan)

Ready to run . . . the mayor changes into comfortable shoes in
preparation for a walk for the March of Dimes in 1984. (*Express-News*
photo by Jose Barrera)

X

High-Tech
and Other Targets

On October 29, 1981, San Antonio's future was in the hands of an eighteen-member board in Austin that was predisposed to keep San Antonio a backwater low-wage town and deny it the chance to compete in a technological age.

The issue was whether the University of Texas at San Antonio would receive approval for a state-supported engineering school. It was up to the all-powerful Coordinating Board of the Texas College and University System to say yes or no, and its members had all but decided to say no.

If newly-elected Mayor Cisneros had any hope at all of keeping his campaign promise to fundamentally alter San Antonio's economy in order to raise wages, then the engineering school was an absolute must. Although San Antonio was the 10th largest city in the United States, the average income level was one of the lowest in the country. In fact, in a 1980 survey of per capita income of the 75 largest cities in the United States, San Antonio ranked 73.

Without a first-rate engineering school offering

degrees in civil, mechanical, and electrical engineering, the new high technology firms that were eyeing Sunbelt cities as potential location sites wouldn't even give San Antonio the time of day.

During the same period of time that John Naisbitt was doing research for *Megatrends* from his office in Washington, D.C., Cisneros was also studying changes in the U.S. economy. Both men reached the same conclusion independently: The United States is moving towards an informational or technology-based economy. Naisbitt showed that in 30 years the U.S. economy had reversed directions. In 1950, 60 percent of Americans were working in industrial jobs and 20 percent were processing information. By the early 1980's, 20 percent of the country's work force was employed in industrial sectors and 60 percent by the informational sector.

"The more I read and got a perspective, the clearer it became to me that the industrial era was fading right before our eyes and that the informational age wasn't something out of Buck Rogers or Star Wars. It's a reality," Cisneros recalled. "I decided the byword for San Antonio had to be diversification. Where do you diversify to? You diversify to a sector that's growing, not one that isn't growing. The steel industry isn't moving. The auto industry isn't moving. Manufacturing is moving some, but selectively. What's growing in this country are the technologies."

Clearly, San Antonio could not hope to carve out a space in its economy for high-tech jobs without an engineering school. Cisneros and leaders of United San Antonio, a peacekeeping coalition of business, government, and the general public which was established at the end of the turbulent 1970's, decided to make an all-out fight for the school. Among those who signed on to do battle were former Mayor Cockrell, executive director of United San Antonio; General Robert F. McDermott, an early leader of USA; and Harold O'Kelley, chairman of the board of Datapoint Corporation.

At McDermott's request, O'Kelley pulled together an engineering education council, whose members concluded that a state-supported engineering school was long over-due in San Antonio. O'Kelley's council found that even if no new businesses located in San Antonio between 1981 and 1985, the city would need a 50 percent increase in engineers.

San Antonio's business community was so alarmed by the findings of the report that O'Kelley quickly set up a foundation which raised $1 million to help endow the proposed school at UTSA. San Antonio was ready to put its money where its mouth was; the city wasn't looking for a handout from the state. However, neither the report nor the endowment drive was enough to convince either the Coordinating Board's study committee or its staff that an engineering school was needed at UTSA. Both the committee and the staff gave the proposed engineering school a negative recommendation.

With two strikes against them, Cisneros, Cockrell, McDermott, and O'Kelley traveled 90 miles up Highway 35 to Austin to present San Antonio's case at a public hearing. The hearing was held in a large room crammed with people from all over Texas who had come hats in hand to the Coordinating Board. Board members have the final word on all degree changes and new construction at state universities. The room was filled with the sound of people shuffling papers, whispering to one another, leaving the room for coffee and coming back again.

Against this background of noise and confusion, San Antonio's delegation tried to make the best possible case. Dr. James Wagener, president of UTSA, pointed out the university had enough land to build an engineering school. O'Kelley told board members about the $1 million endowment fund that San Antonio business leaders had raised to support the school. McDermott hammered away at the critical need for engineers in San Antonio. The well-   121 rehearsed presentation was going as well as could be expected, but the local delegation realized that they were up against tough odds. The coordinating board had a long history of refusing such requests. The official position was that expensive degree programs should not be duplicated: If San Antonio students wanted to pursue engineering studies, they could do it in Austin at the main campus of the University of Texas.

It was that point which Cisneros chose to address in the closing argument. As he started to speak, the restless crowd realized he was talking about more than an engineering school and quickly quieted. He told the board members that he hadn't come to talk to them about engineering but about human lives.

He pleaded with them to allow young San Antonians who are too poor to leave home to attend a university but who possess "latent, pent-up hunger for education" the chance to study to be engineers at UTSA. Then he told them that the decision was not whether to approve or disapprove an engineering school but whether "San Antonio would participate in making the destiny of Texas great or whether San Antonio would become a ward and dependent of the state."

When he finished, the room exploded with applause. The board chairman turned to a staff person seated behind him and asked, incredulously, "What are we going to do now?" The next day, the board voted 14 to 4 to approve a civil, mechanical, and electrical engineering program at UTSA. The first year, 500 students enrolled and the second year, enrollment jumped to 750. Everyone agreed that Cisneros' closing argument had been the decisive factor in the board's decision.

The story illustrates an important point about how Cisneros interprets the role of mayor. In case after case— only occasionally unsuccessfully—what Cisneros has done in San Antonio is define his dream for the city, convince others to buy into that dream, and then focus on

122

action plans to make the dream come true. He not only views himself as San Antonio's strategic planner, but as the primary salesman for the city.

After winning approval of the engineering school, Cisneros went to work writing a detailed action plan for building a major technology sector in the San Antonio economy by the late 1980's. He wrote it while riding around the country on airplanes or late at night in his study at home. He titled it "San Antonio's Place in the Technology Economy" but it quickly became known as simply the "orange book." In the book, Cisneros described the five fastest growing technological sectors in the United States and offered a step-by-step approach to attract industries in those sectors to San Antonio. The "orange book" became a rallying point for all the various economic development groups in town. It also earned Cisneros a national reputation as an expert on the relationship of cities to the changing world economy. In February 1982, Cisneros delivered the Richard S. Childs Lecture to the City Club in New York and spoke about national urban policy.*

In a series for public television, Naisbitt named San Antonio one of the cities to watch in the future and called Cisneros "the best-informed public official on the new information electronic economy that is replacing the older smokestack industrial age." Soon, Cisneros found himself a guest on the *MacNeil-Lehrer Report* talking about the implications of the technological age on urban areas. He wound up speaking on the subject on a variety of Congressional panels.

As a professor of urban affairs, Cisneros has one lecture that is a guaranteed show-stopper. It is always the most popular lecture of any given semester. In the course

---

*The Childs lecture, "A Survival Strategy for America's Cities," is reprinted in its entirety in *Representative American Speeches 1982-1983*, edited by Owen Peterson (H. W. Wilson Company, New York, 1983).

of an hour, Cisneros describes 43 personal lessons that he has learned over the years. Lesson No. 12 is: "Be attentive to details. Lack of such attention will undo 95 percent of your good work. Learn ways to walk through problems and circumstances mentally to train the mind for detail and for pressure situations." Lesson No. 42 is: "Dream big. Be daring enough and free enough to think through scenarios of the future and extend your role in it beyond your present expectations."

With the "orange book," Cisneros practiced what he preaches to students. The results were remarkable, both for Cisneros and the city.

Slowly but surely, the hard work of Cockrell, McDermott, and Cisneros is beginning to pay off. Control Data made a commitment to the inner city in 1979 when the giant computer firm announced the opening of an electronics manufacturing plant in a blighted neighborhood just west of downtown. More manufacturing plants, such as Farinon Electric Company and a Levi Strauss garment plant, broke ground that same year.

Cisneros is pleased with the slow-but-steady growth of manufacturing jobs in San Antonio. He is convinced that the higher the percentage of manufacturing jobs there are in a city, the more equitable the distribution of income among citizens. When he was doing research for his doctoral dissertation in the early 1970's, Cisneros looked at the economic development of 50 cities during a span of six decades. He discovered that the cities which had the highest number of manufacturing jobs had the least disparity in income levels because such jobs traditionally employed blue-collar workers. San Antonio's economy, which is dependent on military bases and tourism, has only 12 percent of its economic base in manufacturing, compared to the average of most cities which is approximately 20 percent.

"What I decided to do was push the city toward a larger manufacturing percentage," Cisneros said recently. "I'm not trying to make us a technology center. I'm trying to diversify the economy around four healthy anchors. The military brings stability in that it is fairly non-vulnerable to recession; tourism also brings that quality of being non-cyclical. The technology sector will bring some growth and some distributional effect. The fourth sector, as I see it now, is medical services, medical research, and medical manufacturing."

Having defined the dream, Cisneros plunged into the implementation of the "orange book." He assigned the book to the Economic Coordinating Council, a group of people who are working on economic development issues through United San Antonio, the Economic Development Foundation, all the chambers of commerce, and various universities. "For the first time, we had an economic plan to work from that everyone was relating to," said Jim Dublin, a San Antonio public relations executive who was deeply involved in the operation of EDF. "Everything that has happened in San Antonio since then really came out of the orange book."

In terms of EDF's work, 1981 was a red-letter year. That was the year such high-tech firms as Advanced Micro Devices, Mark Industries, Tandy Corporation, and Sprague Electric Company announced plans to build manufacturing facilities in San Antonio. In that year alone, more than 5,000 new jobs were created in San Antonio. Some of the companies, such as Tandy and Sprague, decided—at the urging of COPS and Cisneros— to locate in central city areas where the jobs are the most needed.* When EDF brings industrial prospects to town, Cisneros is usually involved in the wooing process. Typ-

*In December 1984, Harcourt Brace Jovanovich, Inc., the largest
 publisher of educational books in the nation, announced plans
 for an $8 million plant, taking over an abandoned central city
 warehouse to remodel and expand. Up to 400 employees will

ically, he meets the airplanes of executives and later wines and dines them.

Meanwhile, Cisneros was meeting with principals and teachers from all of Bexar County's fifteen school districts, trying to convince them to emphasize such areas as logic, computer science, calculus, and technical and scientific writing in their curriculums. In speeches all over Texas, Cisneros said the true test of education in the next decade will be whether schools concentrate on teaching the "three C's" of calculating, computing, and communicating, in addition to the traditional three R's.

Two specific suggestions he made in the "orange book" were for the establishment of two new high schools —one emphasizing technological training and the other focusing on health careers. Both schools became reality. In 1983, San Antonio became the first city in Texas to receive state funding for a new high-technology high school. It is located on the campus of San Antonio College. High school students attend regular classes in the morning at their individual schools, but are bused to SAC in the afternoon for four hours of advanced study in math, computer science, and other technology fields. In May 1983, the first class of 38 students graduated from the high-tech high school. Of 25 honor students in the class, 11 were from poor inner-city school districts. Many won scholarships to first-rate universities such as the Air Force Academy, the Massachusetts Institute of Technology, and Harvard.

The following year, the Northside Independent School District opened a Health Careers High School and 150 students from all of Bexar County's school districts enrolled. Students take the normal courses required for high school graduation in Texas but also receive specialized

operate sophisticated computer and printing equipment including laser scanners. Cisneros had "cemented" the agreement by a visit to HBJ's Florida headquarters.

126

instruction to prepare them for health careers.

In the fall of 1982, Cisneros received a telephone call that his instincts told him was simply too good to be true. He heard that representatives of Microelectronics and Computer Technology Corporation (MCC), a consortium of sixteen national high-tech firms, were scanning the Sunbelt horizons looking for a home. Bill Norris, the visionary chairman of the board of Control Data, had pulled all these high-tech firms together because he became concerned that Japan was getting too far ahead of the U.S. on the development of "fifth generation" computers—programmed not just to perform tasks, but to think and reason. In the beginning, Cisneros didn't know many details about the scope of MCC's artificial intelligence research, but he knew enough to realize that if San Antonio could land MCC, then the city's future as a high-tech center was assured.

Cisneros started talking to Bobby Inman, a retired admiral and former CIA deputy director who had signed on as the chief executive officer for MCC. Then he assembled a group of local heavyweights in McDermott's board room at USAA and started putting together a package of promotion and incentives designed to lure MCC. San Antonio became one of 57 cities under consideration.

When the first cut was made, San Antonio had survived and was one of five cities invited to Chicago to make half-hour presentations to the site selection committee. Two other Texas cities—Dallas and Austin—also made the finals.

This time, not even Cisneros could win over MCC's site selection committee. San Antonio's presentation was good, but no amount of audiovisuals or mortgage loan packages could make up for the fact that MCC was looking for a city with a strong, diversified university to hook up with for research and development. If San Antonio had won its engineering school fight fifteen years earlier, the city might have had a real chance. As it was, Austin won   127

the high-tech prize primarily because of the strong research support the University of Texas and Texas A&M
could join to provide.

When Cisneros realized San Antonio was out of the
running, he employed Personal Lesson No. 23: "Learn the
concept of opportunity costs. You don't lose only by taking
a step backward. You also lose by failing to take a step
forward when it is there to be taken. There is almost no
way to make up such an opportunity."

Instead of taking his marbles and going home to San
Antonio, Cisneros took a step forward and helped Austin
clinch the deal. If he couldn't have MCC in San Antonio,
having it just up the road in Austin was the next best
thing. When MCC's fact-finding team visited Austin
several weeks after the meeting in Chicago, Cisneros was
on hand to help Texas Governor White ease any last-
minute doubts committee members might have had.
When it was all over with and MCC announced its decision
to come to Austin, Cisneros won high praise from White
and other statewide players for helping sell the "Texas
Incentive for Austin" package.

Cisneros came back home and instead of standing
still, he took another step forward and started chasing
biomedicine and biomedical technologies. Instead of
focusing so much energy pursuing high-tech electronics
firms, he decided to play to San Antonio's educational
strength, which is in the biomedical area. While San
Antonio's engineering school isn't mature enough to
attract many research facilities, the city is blessed with
an abundance of laboratories doing biomedical research.
The South Texas Medical Center is in place with the University of Texas Health Science Center as a major anchor
for many public and private hospitals. The Southwest
Research Foundation is one of the largest independent research facilities in the country; it has a genetics department with a twenty-four-person staff doing work in gene

128

splicing and other areas. Various universities and military institutions are also doing medical research.

In order to pull all the researchers together and provide a way to move their discoveries into the marketplace, Cisneros pulled out all the stops to accomplish one of the major goals he'd set out in the "orange book." He set his sights on establishing a research park near the South Texas Medical Center and Southwest Research Foundation where research scientists can provide the "critical mass that will generate new products, new companies, and new jobs.

North Carolina's Research Triangle, located between three major universities, got its first tenant in 1960. Today, the park has expanded to 5,500 acres and 20,000 people work there. A number of local people besides Cisneros had been dreaming of creating a similar park focusing on biotech in the San Antonio area. One of them was Bill Peters, executive director of the San Antonio Medical Foundation. He had tried to sell his board on the idea of establishing a public/private research park on some of the foundation's land near the South Texas Medical Center, but the board didn't think much of the idea when it was first presented.

Peters did not give up. He continued work on the idea in his own quiet way until he met Gerry Cooke, a retired Air Force major general, who had moved to San Antonio and set up a consulting firm which specialized in research parks. The two men teamed up and started talking to people like McDermott at the Economic Development Foundation. Eventually, Cisneros found out about them. The mayor went to the Medical Foundation board and convinced them to take on the research park as their responsibility. At that point, the board hired Cooke as its consultant.

"These two guys were prophets," said Dublin, who at Cisneros' request put together a group of lawyers, accountants, architects, and other professionals to help get   129 the research park off the ground. The group became known as the "Tiger Team," or occasionally just "Henry's guys."

In March 1983, after Cooke and Peters had made a case for the bio-tech park and the "Tiger Team" had pulled together the details of how it would work, Cisneros asked the business community to back the effort with money and land. McDermott was named chairman of the San Antonio Bio-Technology Foundation and went to work raising money and searching for a site. A year later, McDermott and the other members of the board had assembled 1,500 acres of land for the Texas Research Park. Its location in the west quadrant of the city pleased Cisneros because he anticipates that the park will stimulate economic development in the Edgewood Independent School District, one of the poorest school districts in the state.

Since the "orange book" had produced such good results in the economic development area, Cisneros decided to do the same sort of strategic planning with every major issue facing the city. Thus was born Target '90, a comprehensive attempt to involve citizens in setting specific goals to be accomplished by 1990.

More and more, Cisneros became convinced that in this time of technological change, cities that plan will do better than cities that don't plan. Cisneros modeled the Target '90 program after Goals for Dallas, a community goals-setting process begun by then-Mayor Erik Jonsson in the 1960's when Dallas was in a state of drift after the assassination of President John Kennedy.

More than any other exercise, the Target '90 process demonstrated Cisneros' inherent strengths and weaknesses as a politician. While he is good at defining the dream, he grows restless when others are slow to buy into his ideas. Though Target '90 was a success, in that more than 500 widely diverse citizens spent eighteen

months coming up with 170 specific goals for the city,

Cisneros was impatient about selling the idea to his colleagues on the City Council. That caused problems.

Before any citizen groups were brought on board, Cisneros sat down and wrote a draft Target '90 report with his own goals for San Antonio. He presented his goals and unveiled the elaborate Target '90 structure at a kickoff luncheon for his 1983 reelection campaign. Since he won reelection with more than 93 percent of the vote, there was no question that the City Council members were going to have to go along with Target '90 whether they wanted to or not. In an effort to get other council members involved in the effort, Cisneros assigned each council member to one of the twelve Target '90 task forces. Some council members took their assignments seriously; others seem to feel that Target '90 was Cisneros' monument to himself and held back. Since San Antonio operates under a council-manager form of government, the mayor, no matter how popular, can't do so much as hire his own secretary without six votes. If any of the 170 goals spelled out in Target '90 are going to be implemented, Cisneros needs a majority of council members backing both him and the process he set up.

Perhaps the smartest thing he did was name Robert Marbut, the chief executive officer of Harte-Hanks Communications Corporation, as general chairman of Target '90. A heavy thinker himself, Marbut was able to stay one or two mental steps ahead of Cisneros throughout the eighteen-month process, as well as keeping the lid on the unwieldy Target '90 organizational structure. Normally a pragmatist, Marbut found himself in the unusual role of having to convince Cisneros that until the Target '90 task forces agreed upon general, overarching themes, they couldn't come up with specific goals.

"I ended up believing that the process was more important than the plan. You've got to have a process that people buy into before you get down to the nitty-gritty," Marbut recalled.

The mixed signals between Marbut and Cisneros   131

about whether they wanted a general plan or specific goals caused confusion. Trinity University President Ron Calgaard, who was coordinating chairman of the education task force, was one of those frustrated by the process. "You don't write detailed plans of action in huge committees. When you get down to the end, a few experts have to sit down and write specific plans," Calgaard said.

The big question is will Target '90 mean anything or will it be another report to gather dust? The verdict is still out, but on at least one critical vote after the Target '90 report was finished, the City Council chose to ignore the recommendations of a task force.

The issue was city funding for the arts. It was nothing short of miraculous that all the various arts groups got together in the Target '90 task force. Arts groups have been at each other's throats for many years in San Antonio, each trying to do in other groups to get city funds. Not only did the warring groups come together in the Target '90 task force, but they actually agreed upon a set of goals. One of the goals they signed off on was the idea that city funding of arts groups should be depoliticized. They suggested specific criteria be developed to evaluate which artists should receive city funding and which should not, instead of relying on political intrigue.

When the issue of arts funding surfaced during heated discussions of the city budget a few months after the Target '90 recommendations were made public, City Council not only ignored the suggestions of the arts task force but only reluctantly agreed to hear from Joe Krier, its coordinating chairman. "The good news is that Target '90 was an ingenious idea that got a lot of people involved in the city," Krier said. "The bad news is that unless a majority of the City Council gets committed to the goals, they probably aren't going to mean very much."

In late 1984, United San Antonio and the Target '90 Commission merged to form one group that will monitor the implementation of the 170 goals. Nineteen ninety was only six years away.

Whether or not most of the goals become reality may in large part depend on whether San Antonians learn one of those lessons that Cisneros tries to get across to young urban affairs students. Lesson No. 11 in his lecture is: "It is important to realize that there is no millenium when one's task is finished or when the world stands still for a moment of satisfaction. Public issues and problems are dynamic. Change is a dominant characteristic. One's goals, then, have to focus on concepts like dynamism, equilibrium, checks and balances of power, capacity building, due process, and institution building."

The major question for San Antonio is not whether Target '90 produces new highways, airports, and other physical projects, but whether it will produce a new generation of leaders who can follow in Cisneros' very large shoes.

XI

The Democratic Future

Early on the morning after Ronald Reagan's land-slide victory over Walter Mondale in the 1984 election, Mayor Henry Cisneros appeared on the *CBS Morning News* to discuss the lessons for the national Democratic Party.

To be a national party again, he warned, the Democratic Party must compete in all parts of the country and not write off whole regions like the South and West. It must also, he said, be perceived as a broad national party, speaking to national themes. "The Democratic Party that becomes the party of the minorities," he cautioned, "will become a minority party nationally."

If this surprised some observers who saw Cisneros as no more than a spokesman for Hispanics, they had not done their homework. The San Antonio mayor's personal approach to politics has always been as a unifier and coalition-builder, seeking consensus for pragmatic solutions to problems of government and the economy.

He has pursued an agenda that recognizes the inter-ests of the business community as well as populist community organizations—and, in so doing, has held firm control of the broad political mainstream.

His essential message, stressing economic develop-ment, has been non-ideological. As he put it in his post-election appearance on CBS: ["Jobs for everyone in a changing economy . . . is one of those themes that works well for whites, blacks, Hispanics, and everyone else."]

This essential core of the Cisneros approach to pol-itics was obscured during the Democratic National Convention in San Francisco when the San Antonio mayor was employed by the Mondale high command as its emissary to the Hispanic caucus. These 261 delegates were narrowly divided over a proposal that they abstain from voting on the first ballot as a protest against the controversial Simpson-Mazzoli immigration bill.

The Mondale strategists feared that such a boycott would seriously damage his push to win nomination on the first ballot. Mondale had earlier announced his op-position to the bill, which was also opposed by Hispanic leaders, including Cisneros. They were convinced that its provisions for sanctions against employers who hire illegal immigrants would inevitably result in a reluctance to hire Hispanic citizens.

Cisneros joined other major Hispanic elected officials in a session with Mondale and met with AFL-CIO Presi-dent Lane Kirkland at breakfast. The meetings produced new pledges of opposition to the immigration bill and the caucus rejected the boycott proposal on a voice vote—but only after several days of controversy.

Cisneros was chosen to speak at the Tuesday night convention session in support of the justice plank of the Democratic platform. His appearance was late in the proceedings and many delegates had left after hearing the powerful and emotional speech of the Reverend Jesse Jackson earlier in the evening. Still, the mayor's address provided insight into his approach to civil rights and equal opportunity.

135

He opened with a tribute to black civil rights leaders, including Jackson, explaining: "As a Hispanic American who has seen my city change for the better because of the Voting Rights Act, and who has seen children's futures brightened because of our national commitment to equal opportunity, I say sincerely to the black leaders and black community of our nation, thank you, thank you, thank you for the sacrifices and the leadership that have opened up our country for all the rest of us."

Cisneros spoke at length on the Democratic theme of fairness, applying the concept to the plight of unemployed workers in the basic industries of the "rust belt," and pledging that fairness means "that we don't discard old industries or old cities or old people as if they were Coke cans or junk cars." He spoke of fairness in terms of improving the earnings of women workers who collect "a paycheck that is only 70 percent of what a man earns." He invoked opposition to the immigration bill, as he challenged: "Where is the justice for Americans born here in this country, the sons and daughters of men who landed at the Normandy beaches, too, but who are denied work because employers fear that anyone with skin the color of mine or hair that is dark or a last name that sounds like Garcia or Hernandez or Rodriguez *may* be illegal?"

The final words of the Pledge of Allegiance, Cisneros pointed out to applause, do not limit justice to people who live in the right neighborhood or who have the right last name or are born with money. Instead, he emphasized, they promise "liberty and justice for all."

"The speech," Cisneros later told us, "was a minor part of what I did [at the convention]. I wrote it Wednesday afternoon and gave it Wednesday night. I was one in a drowning litany of speakers. My own presentation was distinguished only slightly by the fact that the Texas delegation stayed to hear it."

136   Actually, the mayor's performance at the convention

validated the attention he had received as a result of the vice presidential sweepstakes. His influence was not confined to his efforts for Mondale within the Hispanic caucus. He was invited to speak to delegations with no significant Hispanic influences, including those from Massachusetts, Missouri, and Maine.

He also received high marks from national political writers. In a post-convention appraisal of the party's "emerging stars," William Endicott and George Skelton of the *Los Angeles Times* observed: "One young party official who left here with a much stronger reputation than he had when he arrived was Cisneros, 37, one of the top elected Latino officials in the country and one of only seven persons interviewed by Mondale as a possible running mate."

They added a cautionary note. "But the articulate, Harvard-educated Cisneros," they wrote, "will have to move well beyond the confines of municipal politics to be taken seriously as a national candidate."

It was a reservation that Cisneros-watchers had heard before and would continue to hear. But the mayor made it clear that he was working on a timetable that put city business first. Returning to San Antonio, he reiterated his intention to run for reelection in 1985, telling us: "I have an agenda for our city that will prevent my being available for doing the things I would need to do to run for higher political office. Specifically, the agenda is Target '90."

And he had advice for those who might want to succeed him as mayor, explaining they "would do well to help me with this agenda, not oppose me." The mayor's timetable, however, was not definitive. "I think I can do all this in the next two, three, four, five years," he said. "I intend to stay around and fight for these issues."

Cisneros set limited objectives for his fall campaigning. "I can't deliver Texas," he warned. "I may be able to help in South Texas and I intend to try." The mayor did, indeed, throw himself into campaigning, mostly on weekends, and helped raise the intensity of party workers. But there was no stopping the Reagan tide in Texas, particularly after the state appeared to be written off by the national Mondale organization. Though the great bulk of South Texas counties remained Democratic, Bexar County was part of the Reagan sweep.

Despite the outcome, the mayor's style and personality impressed several of the state's most effective political fund-raisers and they signalled their readiness to sign on with Cisneros when, and if, he decided to make a bid for a major statewide office.

And what about the process of rebuilding the Democratic Party from the 1984 debacle? "I'm probably not going to be as active as I would like," he said in late November. "I would like to jump with both feet into a major party role, but I think that, in form and in structure, my input will be limited to those opportunities when I have a chance to speak and make a presentation." He went on to explain that a full-fledged role would be too time-consuming, and that most decisions will be made in party meetings in Washington, while he will be in the Southwest.

Still, he said, he saw no need to be reticent about his views. "After all, what's at stake is the future of the party and I believe in this party and believe in its basic principles and think there is room for everyone."

The mayor expanded on his immediate post-election remarks, reiterating the need for the Democratic Party to campaign nationally again. Arguing that "some aspects of the political conventional wisdom are valid," he cited ticket-balancing and emphasis on every region of the country. The alternative "is to become a regional party that has lost all of the Western and Midwestern states and the Southern states. There are just too many electoral votes given up if you start the race with a 150 electoral vote deficit."

At a time when "the demographics of the country are moving to the Southwest," he warned, "it's just suicidal strategy to accept regional party status."

Enlarging on his call for the party to seek national themes "that really are positive and unify people," he told of an unsettling phenomenon of the campaign.

"I can't tell you," he said, "how many Anglo males I had approach me in the last weeks, friends saying, 'Henry, you will have to tell me why I should vote Democratic.' I tried to answer the question with references to the history and background of the party. . . . But they wanted to know what, in this present era, the Democratic Party had to offer them."

Cisneros termed this a legitimate question. "We need to again speak to the needs of all the people of the country," he said. Probing the problem further, he observed: "The message of the Democratic Party in terms of compassion and justice and equity is valid. We don't need to back up on that at all. But we do need to find a combination of that message with an understanding of the role that growth in the private sector plays in the economy, the role of defense in global survival, and a practical addressing of the needs of all people, given that the country is becoming generally more prosperous. It's not incompatible that poor people can make progress if the country becomes more prosperous. That's not an incompatible notion at all."

Party leaders must also remember that the Democratic Party is a political party. "There's something to be said for politics," Cisneros argued, "as against what you might call the temptation to lead causes . . . movements. The Democratic Party survived over the years because it is a political party. That sounds on its face as the obvious, but it really says something. A political party is, by definition, engaged in compromise. It's engaged in finding common positions for everyone. That's the business of politics."

Cisneros will have several platforms available for developing his views. He is in the process of writing a 139

CISNEROS

book in which he will discuss the future of the Democratic
Party, as well as relations with Mexico, the Central American problem, cities in the high technology era, and the
role of the Southwest and the Sunbelt in the future of
the country.

He was elected president of the Texas Municipal
League at its meeting in the fall of 1984, a role that will
increase his already-high visibility in the state. And in
late November, 1984, he was selected to be second vice
president of the National League of Cities at its convention in Indianapolis. In due course, he can be expected to
rise to the presidency and assume a lead role as a spokesman for the cities in 1986-87—a remarkably swift rounding
of a full circle by the young graduate student who joined
the League as a staffer in 1970.

Despite his commitment to continue as San Antonio's
mayor, it is clear that Cisneros will have a national audience and he shows promise of reaching out to groups that
were largely indifferent to the party's 1984 message. He
speaks to the values of the fastest-growing segments of
the voting population—Hispanics, of course, but also the
young professionals of the baby boom generation who
are economically sensitive and are attracted to a leader
who can speak with authority on economic development
in the high technology era, while conserving the bedrock
values of the Democratic Party.

What many national politicians have missed is that,
in the words of Texas pollster George Shipley, "Hispanic
life values are among the most traditional, family-orient-
ed, patriotic- achievement- and work-ethic-based of any
group in the country." Cisneros reflects and speaks to
those values, and in so doing, speaks to the values of the
Anglo middle class—the population group that all but
deserted the Democratic ticket in 1984.

In the wake of his defeat, Walter Mondale wryly
confessed what everyone already knew—that he simply
140   could not be comfortable or natural in front of TV cameras,

a fatal flaw in contemporary politics—particularly for opponents of Ronald Reagan—but one shared by many older politicians.

For Cisneros, the TV camera is an ally, and he has learned quickly how to make maximum use of the electronic media. Yet his full potential is just now being perceived by many political players, even in Texas.

"His opponents have always underestimated his resilience, intellect, and depth," says Shipley. "When the going gets rough, he's tight and strong. . . . He is a truly nationally-qualified natural."

Still there remains the question of how and when Cisneros will meet the challenge of moving beyond the City Hall stage to establish his credentials in a major statewide race. In the wake of the 1984 elections, Jerry Hall, a veteran Texas political consultant, took note of the increasing interest in the mayor's plans and asked the familiar question, "He's sitting there in the starting blocks. When is he going to take off?"

That is a question with no easy answer. Since the years when he was a councilman and it was painfully obvious he was preparing to run for mayor, Cisneros has learned to cloak his intentions. Aside from his 1985 race for reelection, his future political agenda is a blank.

In a state as large and complex as Texas, a race for a major office has an incredibly long lead time. To run statewide in 1986, Cisneros would have to begin raising funds and crisscrossing the state early in 1985—a difficult project for a mayor dedicated to converting the promise of Target '90 into reality.

The mayor is a careful and perceptive long-range planner, however. For some years he has been in demand as a speaker before business and professional groups throughout Texas. His election as president of the Texas Municipal League will expand these appearances and strengthen his ties to the network of city officials over the state. And, meanwhile, he has "paid his dues" in the   141

Democratic Party in the bruising campaigns of 1984.

Cisneros is still young enough to wait and build his base for a few years. His timetable seems to point to 1990, an off-year election in which Republican Senator Phil Gramm must face reelection and there is a possibility of open races for governor and lieutenant governor. He is, as *Reader's Digest* observed in December of 1984, "so successful he doesn't *need* to be a young man in a hurry." But if opportunity knocks, Cisneros will move.

In this, as in all politics, timing and luck will be essential ingredients. We can only note that, so far in his career, Cisneros has had a sure sense of timing and an uncanny ability to exploit the breaks that came his way.

No matter what happens to Henry G. Cisneros—or does not happen—his story is already an encouraging one for the future of American politics. He is a politician with high purpose, an idealist who knows the ropes. After a long period of disillusionment with the political process, young people, whether Hispanic or not, can take heart from this example of what can be accomplished with combative energy, enthusiasm, and "the work of one's own hands."

Appendix A:

Speech to American Planning Association annual meeting in Corpus Christi, April 9, 1984.

CITY PLANNING IN THE 1980'S

Because changes are taking place in the role of cities in our society, the role of city planning is changing also. The profession has been marked by changes in at least four significant areas.

1. Strategic Planning

One change involves the role of strategic planning, the guidance of a city at a strategic level. For the planner this role goes beyond the traditional concerns of land use and zoning, beyond those aspects of the profession which deal with design, architecture, and landscaping, and addresses instead issues such as the ebb and flow of economic change in the society at large. In the history of America's cities, planning decisions have enabled cities to change their trajectories in relation to the larger economy. For example, New York City in 1800 was not the premier city in America in terms of its port or trade relationships with England. In that era, Boston was. But Boston suffered from the fact that its hinterland had only limited agricultural potential and as a result it did not have the ability to trade produce after manufactured goods had been shipped from England. When New York's leaders decided in 1803 to construct the Erie Canal, suddenly upstate New York and its more fertile farmland had access to the port. The result was that New York captured and has maintained to this date its role as the premier trading and financial center of the United States. It was a visionary decision, not an accident of geography or random economic chance, that realized the potential of the port of New York.

More recently, in 1900, Houston's leaders made a decision to link their inland city with the Gulf of Mexico by building the ship channel. When the ship channel was linked with the East Texas oil and gas finds, it made possible the development of Houston as an oil and gas

143

technology center. Such a center could have been created at other places along the Gulf Coast, but it was that decision to dig that channel—a bold idea, a visionary concept—that resulted in almost 40 miles of oil refineries and the capital base to start Houston on the road toward becoming the world oil and gas center that it is today.

Still a more recent example: In 1964, Dallas was feeling the community uncertainty that followed the assassination of President Kennedy. That sense of drift was described by Erik Jonsson, who was then the Mayor of Dallas. At first he did not know how to rekindle a sense of enthusiasm and forward motion. He settled on a community goals setting process that came to be known as the Goals for Dallas program. After 20 years it is recognized as the most successful city goals program and is still working today under the aegis of a foundation which last year published a status update of the goals, entitled "The Possible Dream." As part of the Goals for Dallas effort, identification of the need for a "port to the ocean of the air" resulted in the DFW Airport, the air transportation hub of the Southwest. It could have been in other cities. The airlines were looking for a central location—Tulsa, Oklahoma City, Kansas City—that could serve as the exchange point for traffic in the southwestern states. But because the need was recognized, because the community consensus was built, because the project was undertaken, DFW is that point.

Small cities can respond by making strategic changes also. Lowell, Massachusetts, lost its textile industry 20 years ago. Today it is a thriving city on the basis of two actions: (1) a historic preservation effort that led to downtown revitalization, and (2) the attraction of technology jobs to settings compatible in scale and character with the historic setting. Wang Laboratories are operating today in a restored textile mill in Lowell. Fort Wayne, Indiana, is another example. Fort Wayne was recognized nationally by USA Today as the "most livable small city in America" less than two years after the closing of a Caterpillar plant. In the same year, it won an All-American City award for the civic responses that had been brought to bear in Fort Wayne in that short time.

In San Antonio today we are taking a crack at community involvement in the strategic planning process. We call our effort TARGET '90. It is an attempt to sort through some 170 goals and identify those which we can reasonably accomplish by 1990. A scant six years from now, in some 70 months, it will be 1990. To officials engaged in the day-to-day pressures of city government, it seems a long time from today. But it is hardly enough time to plan a freeway or to build a downtown mall where acquisition of land, design issues, and working drawings can easily dictate a time frame of six years or more. It is hardly enough time to persuade a university to start a new engineering curriculum or enough time to see improvements in standardized test scores as a result of public school innovations. In any event, that is the time frame we chose because we found that our citizens could relate to a deadline which was sufficiently distant to allow for initiative and flexibility but not so far as to be unimaginable. Some 500 citizens have been involved for more than a year in reviewing goals for the future of our community.

City planners all over America are having to do some strategic thinking in this time of technological change, in this time of decentralization of responsibilities out of Washington and beyond state capitals. Local governments that plan in this way will do better than those that do not. Cities that have a vision of where they want to go will do better than those that have not thought about it. Cities that organize themselves to anticipate change will do better than those that do not. It is a very simple proposition, but most communities, for political or other reasons, do not address themselves to a strategic framework—to the great changes moving across our country.

2. Economic Development

A second dimension of the expanding role of city planning is more clearly in the economic realm. It has to do with city governments as major actors in the economic development process. In my judgment, the central issues 145 for cities through the rest of this century—whether in the Northeast where the economic direction is decline or in the Southwest where the dynamic is growth—will be jobs and the equity considerations attendant on extending economic participation to all in the society. Even in the growth environment that characterizes Texas today, the challenge of assuring equity and maintaining the quality of life will absorb the attentions of city officials. Today in Texas there are 14 million people, and it is estimated that by 1995 there will be more than 20 million. That increase in population will require a 50% increase in the capacity of the public facilities in this state—be it expressways, schools, hospitals, universities, or hotel and convention facilities. It is not a question of whether it will occur, nor is it a question of when. It is only a question of how we prepare for that growth and what we want to accomplish, because it will occur in our state.

A major task for planners will be to understand the functioning of cities in the economic arena. The training of planners for the rest of this decade will require definition of the economic "macro" picture and "micro" detail as well. Jobs will be the central issue before elected leaders as the Texas economy makes the transition out of its dependence on oil and gas and as cities attempt to diversify. Planners who want to understand where the elected officials are going need to be thinking in terms of jobs, incomes, and economic development.

San Antonio, on the basis of new census estimates, is now ranked the 10th largest city in America. This makes Texas the only state in more than 100 years to have three cities among the ten most populous cities in the country. The last time that occurred was in 1865 when New York State had Brooklyn (then an independent city), New York City, and Buffalo in the top ten. Now it has happened again and the fact serves as well as any other statistic as a capsule summary of the dynamic that is underway. But Texas' growth is not just a big-city phenomenon. In the 1970's, of the 15 fastest growing small metropolitan areas in America, six were in Texas—places such as McAllen, Bryan-College Station, and Longview.

There are also some qualitative economic changes occurring in Texas, quite apart from the numerical increases in growth statistics. Some of those changes should be of interest to the planning profession. The base of the Texas economy is changing. No longer will we be able to be as reliant on the oil and gas industry as we have been. No longer will we be able to function in the belief that the Texas economy is invulnerable to national recessions. The mythic "boom forever" will simply not extend into the future.

1983 was a year to begin to understand that reality. It was the year a "triple whammy" bludgeoned the Texas economy. First came the national recession. It bottomed-out, economists now say, in October-November of 1982, when national unemployment exceeded 10%. In Texas the low point came a little later, but it hit with unprecedented force. Despite our traditional characterization of the Texas economy as recession-proof, the Texas economy today resembles the national economy in terms of its diversity. There is, for example, more manufacturing in Texas than ever. As a result, when there is a recession nationally, Texas feels it—and will feel every recession in the future.

The second shot in the "triple whammy" was the down-turn in oil and gas prices. Anyone who worked in the "oil patch" cities—Houston, Beaumont, Port Arthur, Corpus Christi, Odessa, Midland, or in smaller communities such as Alice where production activity fell off—knows it. Many parts of Texas well know what it means when the base of the economy is in a slump. For example, it has meant very high office vacancy rates and high unemployment in Houston. Houston never had an unemployment rate higher than 5% throughout the decade of the 1970's, but its rate reached 9.7% in June 1983.

The third shot in the "triple whammy" was the peso devaluation in Mexico. It is virtually impossible to describe in words the devastation and human suffering caused by the peso devaluation among Texas communities in the border regions. It is difficult for most Americans to comprehend the effects of 30% unemployment in Lare-   147 do, in Del Rio, and in Eagle Pass, cities where the main economic transactions revolve around border trade. The practical result of the depression caused by the devaluation is that people are turning in their homes to the banks, returning their automobiles, and moving in with relatives as unemployment compensation benefits run out.

A fourth problem—the weather—intensified the "triple whammy" in 1983: the heat and the drought on the High Plains in the summer months and then the record-breaking freeze of December. In the Rio Grande Valley the freeze destroyed not only the citrus orchards but also the food processing industry, terminating 40,000 jobs.

1983 was a rough year for Texas. But it was also the year in which the first signals of a major new direction for the Texas economy were observed. The MCC decision was announced in Austin and Texans began to focus on the potential for a technology future for Texas. It was also the year when the state leadership devoted its strongest political energies to education. Governor Mark White, Ross Perot, the Speaker, the Lieutenant Governor, the teachers' unions were stressing education as never before.

3. Economic Infrastructure

A third dimension of the planner's role in this time of technology transition concerns the "new infrastructure" of economic development. In the past, the infrastructure of economic development has been physical assets such as ports and docks, rail facilities and bridges for moving heavy equipment and raw materials, and access to iron ore and nearby coal seams. The business of economic development was the creation of a setting for manufacturing and the basic industries. But the "new infrastructure" of the technology age is less a set of physical assets than it is the ability to create an environment in which leading-edge research can be matched to entrepreneurial capital.

It is, first and foremost, quality education at all levels: good primary and secondary education, targeted vocational education, flexible and effective junior college programs, excellent higher education, and pioneering graduate programs. While every community clearly

148

cannot have nationally-ranked graduate programs, communities can do a lot in technology and vocational education using junior college facilities which, after all, have the immense advantage of being decentralized, capable of innovation, and generally flexible enough for timely response in most communities.

Research institutions should be encouraged to attract the critical mass of talent that can then transform itself into technology product lines in start-up companies. Creating low-density, research campus environments for such companies is an increasingly active area of municipal endeavor. Learning the language of venture capital and seed capital, financing which allows business start-ups to spin off from research and educational institutions, is a priority for city officials today. Attracting foreign technology investments is likely to be an increasingly important strategy for securing investment in urban areas.

Creating institutions to support technology exports is still another part of the business of cities in the 1980's. Phoenix has managed to create a setting in which some 60% of the small and medium-sized businesses that can export are doing so. This is a phenomenal benefit because jobs can be created in small businesses faster than the time generally required to attract a new business to the community. Working to enhance state policies toward technology is another effort in which city leaders must be engaged. Streamlining municipal procedures demonstrates a responsive capability and willingness to act. All of these must become the professional skills of mayors, city council members, planning directors, and planners who will have to build the new infrastructure.

This does not mean that every city can or should join the pursuit of new technology jobs—far from it. But the facts are increasingly clear that the new infrastructure will be needed to support whatever direction is sought for a community. Communities should build to their strengths, analyze their assets, set targets, and then work toward their goals. In every community the strategy will differ, but recognition of the importance of the new infrastruc-   149 ture in the context of strategic planning is going to be essential for cities that want to expand their job base in the technology era.

4. Demographic Change

A fourth dimension of the planner's role is at the nexus of economic transition and the changes in the racial and ethnic character of the nation's cities. Every city in Texas will be affected by demographic change. In the cities of South Texas where there are large Hispanic populations, there will be more Hispanic elected officials. In East Texas, where there are large numbers of persons in Black communities, there will be larger numbers of Black elected officials. We will see minority political and economic participation increase in Waco and Amarillo, in Lubbock and Odessa, in Dallas and Houston. In most places we will see participation by persons who have not had access to power before. One of the critical questions for our cities is whether such transitions can occur in ways that are cooperative, reasoned, and characterized by due process or whether in most cases they must be difficult, hostile, and adversarial.

The question of transition leadership, joint leadership, cooperative leadership, is at the heart of how our cities develop. Planners must seek the involvement of people in participatory ways, recognizing new models of governance. One of the most interesting new models is the so-called "IAF" network, the Industrial Areas Foundations organizations, which in San Antonio is COPS, in Houston is TMO, in El Paso is EPISO, and in the Texas Valley is Valley Interfaith. We will see more neighborhood efforts like the neighborhood movements in Dallas, Fort Worth, and Austin. But the goals of grass-roots oriented people with a desire for participation are not always coterminous with those of the elected officials. In San Antonio it has been tough slugging every step of the way in the relationship with COPS and neighborhood organizations. We are going to see more of that in South Texas.

The answer is not in confrontation, obstruction, or
150 denying of access, but rather in inclusion, cooperation,

providing facts, and trying to build a common stake in the future. In our city of San Antonio that is the second purpose of TARGET '90. Apart from setting goals for the city, TARGET '90 involves bringing people into the process and providing them a stake in the mainstream current of the community. So that when change does occur, as it naturally will, then at least the people have understood and participated in the system for development of the community. That is the dual agenda of TARGET '90: strategic planning, economic development, and preparing for the future by building this new infrastructure; and recognizing the increasingly bicultural or multicultural, sensitive transition that many of our cities are experiencing. . . .

Appendix B:

Democratic National Convention, San Francisco, Tuesday, July 17, 1984.

GOVERNOR DUKAKIS [Mass.]: . . . And to speak also to the Justice segment of the Platform, a young man whom we have been reading a lot about and hearing a lot about these past few weeks, who was a very serious possibility for the vice presidential selection; a young man who went to school in my home state, and is now serving so ably in the State of Texas, and I told him that it was about time we had a little Spanish on this Platform, so senores y senoras, es para mi un gran placer de presentar a la Convencion Democratica y a todos ustedes un hombre joven, inteligente, fuerte, un hombre con un futuro grande, el Alcalde de San Antonio, Texas, Henry Cisneros. (Applause)

PLATFORM PRESENTATION BY MAYOR HENRY G. CISNEROS, SAN ANTONIO

MAYOR CISNEROS: Muchisimas gracias, Governor, y gracias, mis amigos. Thank you very much. Thank you.

My task this evening is to speak about justice. But it would be impossible to talk about justice without saying a word about what we have heard tonight and over the last six months from the Reverend Dr. Jesse Jackson. As a Hispanic American who has seen my city change for the better because of the Voting Rights Act, and who has seen children's futures brightened because of our national commitment to equal opportunity, I say sincerely to the Black leaders and the Black community of our Nation, thank you, thank you, thank you for the sacrifices and the leadership that have opened up our country for all the rest of us. (Applause)

Dr. King used to say that all America would be better because of what he was trying to do. Today, we know that countless thousands of women, Hispanics, Asian Americans, disabled persons, Native Americans and working people are better off because there was a civil rights move-

152

ment, because the Black community set the course for 20 years of change and because Jesse Jackson ran for the Presidency of the United States in 1984. (Applause)

Political change is always difficult to make, but it is made by those who are willing to push at the margins, step out into that territory where no one has been before. It is boggy, it is murky, it is swampy, it is not clear what is out there but those who are willing to take the step into that swampy territory often find that the ground is very solid indeed, and generally it is most solid when the ground has been based on solid truths—on simple, clear, understandable truths.

One of those truths is the idea of justice in our system, fairness in our lives. When I first became the Mayor of San Antonio in 1981, I remember a man about 80 years old who stopped me on the street one day. He had all the signs on his face of weathered wisdom, a gentleman who had worked hard, and he said to me, "Mr. Cisneros, we have had a troubled time. It has been difficult. We have suffered badly. But please, we are not asking for revenge, or hostility, or anger. Just do a good job, and be fair."

People understand fairness. People also understand unfairness, and they know which political Party in this country is more likely to be fair to average folks. It is the Democratic Party. (Applause)

They also know that this campaign is about fairness; and so I ask you, where is the fairness, where is the justice for a Youngstown, Ohio, or Pennsylvania steel worker who has worked his whole life, lives in one of those triple-decker houses, saved his money, tried to put his children through college, lived so that he can retire on Social Security; where is the justice when they tell him the plant is leaving, and Social Security is bankrupt?

This Administration tells him: vote with your feet. Go somewhere to the southwest, maybe Phoenix, and you can be a custodial worker, or you can be a computer programmer. Where is the justice in that?

Fairness means in our country that we don't discard old industries or old cities or old people as if they were Coke cans or junk cars. We need to keep those steel plants,   153 yes, because they are important to the economic recovery, and yes, because they are important to our national defense, but mostly because they are for people; they provide jobs for people, and when we talk about justice, that is what we are talking about. We are talking about an America that has room for all its people.

What is fair to a woman who gets up early every morning, organizes her family's breakfast, works at a job all day, comes home to cooking and the kids' homework— managing her time better than most corporate executives do—and at the end of the month she collects a paycheck, at the end of the month she collects a paycheck that is only 70 percent of what a man earns? (Applause)

And when our Party makes a commitment to fairness for women and puts it into action by nominating a woman to the second highest job in America, what does the President say? He calls her a token. Mr. President, where I come from, any person who works her way through law school at night, raises a family, holds her own in a tough job and gets elected to Congress ain't no token. (Applause)

This Administration, seems to say to women, you have come a long way, baby. Stick with me, and well, maybe someday I will make you somebody.

Democratic women say, Mr. President, as long as a woman earns only 70 percent of a man's pay, we haven't come a long way, and don't call us "baby." (Applause)

My friends, where is the justice for Americans born here in this country, the sons and daughters of men who landed at the Normandy beaches, too, but who are denied work because employers fear that anyone with skin the color of mine or hair that is dark or a last name that sounds like Garcia or Hernandez or Rodriguez may be illegal? Where is the justice in the conditions that will prevail if Simpson-Mazzoli passes and becomes the law of this country? President Reagan is for Simpson-Mazzoli. Our Platform is against it, and all three of our prospective nominees for the presidency have said they are against it.

That same bill would create temporary workers; the

so-called rent-a-slave provisions of that bill would relegate temporary workers to another world of unsanitary and unsafe housing. Instead of further crushing blows against the men and women who labor in 100 percent sun from dawn to dark, fairness says we should be rallying behind Cesar Chavez and his new grape boycott once again. (Applause)

Fairness in our lives, justice in our system. We teach our children in this country when they are four and five years old; when they first go to kindergarten, before they know what the words mean, they accept what we teach them, and what we teach them is the Pledge of Allegiance, and its closing lines say that we are: ". . . one Nation, under God, indivisible, with liberty and justice for all."

It doesn't say justice for some. It doesn't say justice if you are born in the right neighborhood. It doesn't say justice for you if you are born with the right last name. It doesn't say justice for you if you are born with a little money. What it says is liberty and justice for all. (Applause)

But a Nation is more than written words. What it really takes is a commitment to action, and action is what Senator Robert Kennedy told us about in a very favorite quotation of mine from him. It is not one of his more quoted. I found it in a musty stack of some of his speeches, but it captures the essence of people committed to translate words and theory into actions. He said, "It is the shaping impulse of America that it is neither fate nor chance nor the irreversible tides of history that determine our destiny as individuals or as a people. Rather, it is reason and it is principle, and it is the work of our own hands."

He went on to say, "There is pride in that, even arrogance, but there is also truth, and in any event, it is the only way we can live. It is not fate, it is not chance, it is not some invisible hand. It is not a random toss of the dice. It is not irreversibility of history that determines our destiny. It is reason, what we know in our heads. It is principle, what we believe. And finally, it is the work of our brains and our perspirations and our energies and our own hands." And the work of our hands, in the year of   155

1984, is to win a Democratic victory so that justice and fairness may prevail in our land once again.

Thank you very much. (Applause)

INDEX TO TEXT
(Photographic references are not included.)

157

159